MURDER ON THE DARK WEB

TRUE TALES FROM THE DARK SIDE OF THE
INTERNET

EILEEN ORMSBY

CONTENTS

Edited versions of the two stories in this book were first released by the author as scripts for the Casefile True Crime podcast.

Dark Webs True Crime

St Kilda Vic 3182

Australia

PRAISE FOR EILEEN ORMSBY'S BOOKS

'Ormsby has delivered a triumph of narrative journalism, meticulously researched and gripping, a skilful mergence of tech jargon with human drama.' *The Saturday Paper*

'The book is a fascinating expose of this particular aspect of the "dark web" of internet dealings and its subsequent unravelling.' *Sydney Morning Herald*

'Ormsby's investigative journalism shines as she provides a very thorough account of Ulbricht's rise and fall.' *Penthouse Magazine*

'What pulls you through The Darkest Web isn't its often-nefarious, sometimes-gory details, but Ormsby's handling of three progressively intense narrative arcs.' *The Guardian*

'The darkness has become a repository for human cruelty, perversion and psychosis, and Ormsby captures all the tragedy in her gripping book.' *The Australian*

'A great strength of the meticulously researched Silk Road is the manner in which Ormsby gently takes the reader by the hand, unpacking the technology underpinning this 'dark net' market.' *Australian Police Journal*

'A disillusioned corporate lawyer turned writer from Australia, Eileen's new book, The Darkest Web, is the story of her journey, from drug markets and contract killing sites to the Internet's seediest alcoves. But the most startling moments of the book happen when she comes face-to-face with some of its key players.' *VICE*

'From the Internet's hidden drug dens to torture-porn websites, Ormsby has seen it all. If you've ever wondered what the Dark Web is really like, Darkest Web should be on your TBR.' *Bustle Magazine "The Best New True Crime Books You Can Read Right Now"*

'Riveting.' *Who Magazine*

'Investigative journalism that gallops along at a cracking pace.' *SMH Good Weekend*

'Through her clear rendering of the facts, Ormsby makes the intricacies of the technology involved accessible to even the most technophobic of readers. The tone is conversational and friendly while the content is intriguing and increasingly dark. In her quest to uncover the mystery behind the enigmatic DPR she uncovers a story of subterfuge, replete with conspiracy theories and hidden identities, that is rich with anecdotes.' *Newtown Review of Books*

For the Casefile fans
But especially for Casey McCaseFace himself

ABOUT THE AUTHOR

Eileen Ormsby is a lawyer, author and freelance journalist based in Melbourne, Australia. Her first book, *Silk Road*, was the world's first in-depth expose of the black markets that operate on the dark web. In *The Darkest Web*, Eileen's gonzo-style investigations led her deep into the secretive corners of the dark web where drugs and weapons dealers, hackers, hitmen and worse ply their trade. Many of these dark web interactions turned into real-world relationships, entanglements, hack attempts on her computer and even death threats from the dark web's most successful hitman network.

Eileen started writing scripts for *Casefile True Crime Podcast* in 2018 and has since become one of their most regular contributors. She often focuses on cases that have a dark web or internet aspect to them.

PART I

THE DARK WEB

A BRIEF INTRODUCTION TO THE DARK WEB

Anyone who spends any amount of time online would, by now, have heard of the dark web. It is hidden from regular users, only accessible by downloading special software that provides a portal to the websites in this parallel online world. It is the Wild West of the internet, a place where anything goes. Illegal goods are bought and sold, hitmen advertise their services, hackers gather to share data and tips, and forums bring together extremists of every flavor, from anarchists to communists, and terrorist sympathizers to neo-Nazis and white supremacists.

After hiding in the shadows for years, the dark web burst into the headlines thanks to the multimillion-dollar darknet markets. These are online bazaars, which look familiar to anyone who has ever shopped online. Photographs of items for sale entice shoppers to click for more information, and reviews from previous customers and a rating out of five for the seller ensure a smooth experience. There may be bulk discounts, sales or giveaways to attract new customers. There is a resolution center to mediate disputes between buyers and sellers. In the top right-hand corner, there is a familiar shopping cart, ready to be filled with purchases and shipped to anywhere in the world.

The difference is that this cart can be filled with cocaine, ecstasy or heroin. The pictures shoppers are invited to click on are of drugs and weapons, counterfeit cash, fake passports and drivers' licenses. Instead of providing a credit card or PayPal details, shoppers need to acquire cryptocurrency, which allows person-to-person payments without going through a bank or financial institution and where neither person needs to know the other's identity.

Buying drugs from the dark web has increased in popularity every year since Silk Road, the first major point-and-click drugs market, set up shop in 2011. Silk Road advertised itself as an online market where you could buy any drug imaginable. Although Silk Road is long gone, there are now over a dozen such marketplaces, turning over hundreds of millions of dollars selling drugs to people who would prefer to transact online than meet a dealer in real life.

Other sites that can be found on the dark web include political dissent and hate sites, hacking, phreaking or social engineering communities, and pages for every conspiracy theory imaginable. Many sites require an invitation to view them, so their contents remain a mystery.

At the more extreme end, there are sites that claim to trade in human organs or exotic animals. Some offer access to real-life Gladiator fights to the death or live streaming of pay-per-view torture and murder, better known as "red rooms." Services offered on the dark web include theft-to-order, university papers researched and written, insider trading and fixing of sporting events, SWATting (arranging for a SWAT team to raid the house of someone you have a beef with) and an array of hacking services, from social media accounts to bypassing sophisticated business firewalls.

The dark web is essentially a place where the visitor can't discover where the host is and the host can't discover where the visitor is coming from. Nobody—including the organizations that provide access to the sites—can determine who runs them or where they are located. The most disturbing sites are those that offer illegal pornography files and videos, including child exploitation, animal abuse, rape and revenge porn. Hundreds of these sites are able to openly run and advertise for new members, as there is no ISP that law enforcement can insist provide them with information. Nor is there any magic switch that can close them down.

That's not to say that these sites never get shut down or the people behind them identified and prosecuted. Silk Road ran for nearly three years before its owner was unmasked following an investigation that involved law enforcement agencies from around the globe. International taskforces work tirelessly to locate the criminals behind child exploitation sites and track down the perpetrators of the abuse. However, they rely on mistakes made by the criminals, because dark web technology exists to protect the felons from those who hunt them.

Although the terms dark web, deep web and darknet are often used interchangeably, they have different meanings. For example, you might have heard that 90% of the internet is hidden and is part of the deep web. This is true, but it is nothing to be afraid of. The *deep web* is everything you can't find with a search engine like Google. It includes pages behind paywalls, password-protected information, the private parts of your social media accounts, or closed intranets. Personal information that only you can access though your bank's website, for example, is part of the deep web. The content of the deep web is available to anyone who knows the URL (web address) or IP address where it is located, but may require a password or other security measures to access it any meaningful way.

The *dark web* is one tiny part of the deep web, but to view it you need to download a darknet. A *darknet* is like a portal, or road, to the dark web. The most popular darknet is called Tor. It is free, readily available and perfectly legal to use. Its main purpose is to provide anonymity services to anyone who wants them. It is a tool that has been effectively implemented to circumvent the great firewall of China.

Many people have taken the plunge through the portal to browse this underground world. Most merely look around, happy to simply satisfy their curiosity before leaving, never to return. But some are sucked into the criminal underworld and find themselves doing things they would never have contemplated in the real world—ordering a hit on a love rival or bidding on an auction for a sex slave.

Just like the people in this book.

DARK WEB USERS SHARE SOME OF THEIR EXPERIENCES OF THE DARK WEB ON SOCIAL MEDIA

"Murder rooms or "Red rooms" are live video feeds that show the slow and often gruesome murder of someone. Like torture rooms people can pay to have something done to them (appendages removed, skin sliced off, stabbed, etc) except torture rooms have much more options and are not to kill but cause agony (electricity, water boarding, filleting, rape, strangulation, resuscitation, etc)"

- Reddit post

"The dark web is full of shit you don't want to be associated with. Child porn Murder rooms Drugs runners Weapons dealers Hitmen Torture rooms Spy cameras And its very risky. If you don't have proper protection hackers can obtain alot of

information and track you down to your
exact address. Its how alot of Red Rooms
get their victims."

   - Reddit post

—————

"The most disturbing site we found was a
comprehensive guide for cooking women.
We're not talking about a short joke here.
This page had information on what body
types to use for specific cuts, how to
prepare these cuts, and how to cook the
girl so she lives as long as possible."

   — Reddit post

—————

"I downloaded Tor and within 20 minutes of
downloading it and browsing random shit
I got a phone call but there was no one
there and they just hung up after 10
seconds. I didn't even know if it was legal
at the time so that was enough to freak me
out and I stopped right there."

   — Reddit post

—————

"One thing that stuck around was a site
selling military weapons. They had
everything you could think of. I really

wanted the tripod mounted grenade launcher with automation package."

— Reddit post

"There have been many instances on the deep web where users have repeatedly found terrifying live streams. Some guy stumbled on a livestream where a girl was sitting in a chair and commanded people from the chat window to tell her what kind of abuse she should do to herself. After many cuts, bruises, eye gouging, the girl eventually killed herself on the livestream."

— Reddit post

MYTHS AND MURDER

Becuse of the nature of the dark web, stories and rumors swirl around the regular internet, making it difficult to separate fact from fiction. As there is no limit to what can be uploaded onto the dark web, many sites are merely hoaxes. Take, for example, one of the most famous dark websites, *The Human Experiment*, where deranged medical professionals document Nazi-esque experiments carried out on homeless people. Upon arriving at the site, visitors are greeted with this:

The Human Experiment

In this website, we attempt to illustrate several experiments that are being conducted by our group on human subjects. The people chosen for this range of experiments are usually homeless people that are unregistered citizens.

Experimentations range from:

- *Starvation and water/fluid restriction*
- *Vivisection/pain tolerances*
- *Infectious diseases and organ effects*
- *Transfusions*
- *Drug trials*
- *Sterilization*
- *Neonate and infant tolerances to x-rays, heat, and pressure.*

Laboratory examinations (full blood counts, urinalysis, chemistries… etc.) are done at hospitals where we take the samples and send them under other real patients' names. The results are carefully dispersed so as not to arouse suspicion.

The bodies of the dead are dissected and then disposed of in dumpsters of meat shops where their bodies will not be found.

No IRB approval was sought for this secret range of experimentations.

Although *the Human Experiment* site exists and can easily be found on the dark web, there is no evidence that the experiments are anything more than fantasies dreamed up by someone with an overactive imagination. A lot of the tales about the dark web are just creepy fiction, campfire tales for the digital era. Stories like those taken from Reddit earlier in this chapter are just that: stories. They never happened, or were hoax sites. Anyone looking for red rooms, secret government files, human experiments, proof of extraterrestrials or forbidden knowledge invariably comes away disappointed.

However, although there are a lot of myths and misconceptions about the dark web, the darknet markets are very real and turn over hundreds of millions of dollars a year, and many other sites depict and enable actual heinous crimes to be committed on very real victims.

This book looks into two such true crimes. The first is a murder that was ordered through the most profitable dark web murder-for-hire site that ever existed, Besa Mafia. The second story is about an Instagram glamour model kidnapped to be put up for sale by the Black Death group, a shadowy organization specializing in a range of crimes including human trafficking.

These are the true tales of *Murder on the Dark Web*.

PART II

THE MURDER OF AMY ALLWINE

A DEATH IN COTTAGE GROVE

On November 13, 2016, Sergeant Gwen Martin was one of the Cottage Grove police detectives who answered a call to attend an apparent suicide by gunshot wound to the temple. Gwen was just starting the night shift, and the call made her drop everything and rush to 110th Street South, where the call had been placed from. The drive was little more than five minutes, but it seemed to take much longer. The whole ride, the veteran police officer told herself: *This isn't possible. There must be some mistake.*

The address was at the end of a long, dark country road with no streetlights. As Gwen approached in the patrol car, it was easy to spot the first responders lighting up the road at the last house on the right. As she pulled in to the driveway at number 7624, a silver-haired man and a young boy waited outside the house, sheltering in the open garage. The boy wore earmuffs, although winter had not yet set in. Lights inside the house glowed softly, as the blue and red lights from the emergency vehicles strobed outside, illuminating the end of the cul-de-sac.

Gwen entered through the garage and joined three

patrol officers who had already searched the house and located the victim. Amy Allwine lay near the door of the marital bedroom, not yet cold, in a pool of blood. She was on her back, arms out to her sides, unfocused eyes staring into the distance. Gwen was a veteran patrol cop with over eighteen years on the force. As an experienced paramedic, she could handle pretty much anything that the job threw at her. But this time, as soon as she had ordered the younger officers to secure the premises, Gwen handed over to a more junior member of the force and took herself outside.

Gwen Martin knew Amy Allwine. Amy was a happy, successful local businesswoman with a husband and a nine-year-old son. She was part of Gwen's Citizen Police Academy class that had graduated just a couple of weeks earlier. Amy had taken the course in part because she wanted to assist her community, as she always did, wherever she could. But Gwen knew there was another reason Amy had taken the course.

Amy Allwine had been living in fear for the past six months.

A DARK WEB MURDER PLOT

Six months earlier

In the spring of 2016, Detective Sergeant Randy McAlister was sitting in his office at the Cottage Grove Police Department, where he had worked for nearly twenty years. Randy knew that if a man was going to be a police officer, he could do a lot worse than be stationed at Cottage Grove, Minnesota. Cottage Grove, population 36,000, lay on the north bank of the Mississippi River, a half-hour drive from the Minneapolis city center. It had its share of problems, just like any other suburb of a major metropolitan area, but nothing like the problems of the inner city. The municipal offices that housed the police force were large, modern and comfortable. The workload was reasonable and consisted of the usual array of petty crimes and domestic disputes, which could be dealt with routinely and with little danger to the officers themselves.

Randy liked the quiet and predictability of working for a low-crime, small-city community. Serious violent crime was rare, and over his entire career, Randy knew of just two murders, both of which had been in the previous four years.

In both cases, the victim and perpetrator knew each other and he didn't think it was indicative of a future trend of an increase in local homicides.

May 31, 2016 was much like any other day, until the monotony was broken up by a visit by the FBI. Although not an everyday occurrence, it was not completely out of the ordinary for the FBI to contact local police as a courtesy to let them know that they were investigating a crime in their area. Still, it was novel enough that Randy's interest was piqued.

Special Agent Asher Silkey, from the FBI's Minneapolis field office, told Randy that the Bureau had intercepted a threat on the internet involving a resident of Cottage Grove. Asher asked if a local police officer could accompany him to notify the potential victim.

Threat reports were one of the more commonplace issues that police had to deal with and, these days, they invariably came via the internet and text messaging. It could be hard to take them seriously or gather enough evidence to lay any charges. This had to be pretty serious to warrant a personal visit from the FBI rather than a phone call.

Indeed, this threat was a little different—it had come via something called the "dark web." It was a term that Randy had heard but, like most people, didn't really have much understanding of. The FBI agent explained that anything on the dark web was untraceable, but there were enough details contained within the threat itself that the victim was sure to know where it had come from. Randy assigned one of his detectives, Terry Raymond, to accompany Asher to visit Mrs. Amy Allwine at her home at 7624 110th Street South, Cottage Grove.

1 10th Street was a long, semi-rural road of very large blocks. The Allwines lived in the last house on the right before a tiny carpark that led to the Grey Cloud Dunes sand-gravel prairie. The prairie was popular with walkers and sunset watchers would often sit in parked cars, enjoying the view. The letterboxes along the street were peppered with Neighborhood Watch stickers, but there were rarely any incidents that required reporting to the local police.

The house owned by Stephen and Amy Allwine was no shack, but their simple dwelling could not compete with the significantly larger and more elaborate homes of the neighbors. It was the epitome of the worst house on the best street. A pre-fab affair that had been shipped in pieces and assembled on the property, it comprised four small bedrooms, an open-plan kitchen/living area and three bathrooms. An attached double garage provided an alternative entry to the house, via a mudroom that doubled as a laundry.

The twenty-eight acres also held a large barn that had been used for a small manufacturing business, but had been refurbished to house Amy Allwine's dog training business, Active Dog Sports. The rest of the land was rented out for truck gardening.

When Detective Raymond and Special Agent Silkey knocked on the door of number 7624, it was answered by a thin, blond man in his early forties. He was Stephen Allwine, he explained, and he worked from an office in the basement. His wife, Amy, was not home. The two law enforcement officers told him they needed to speak to her urgently; they could not provide details, but assured Stephen they did not think she was in immediate danger.

They made arrangements for Amy to attend the Cottage Grove Police Department as soon as she could the next day.

On June 1, 2016, Stephen and Amy Allwine dutifully turned up to the police station. When the FBI agent told them why they had been called in, the story that unfolded was unbelievable.

———

The Cottage Grove police had to educate themselves about what exactly the dark web was. They learned the dark web was a sort of parallel internet, an evil twin of sorts, that can only be accessed by downloading special software. Once it is installed on a computer, a user can visit websites that can't be found on the regular internet. Sites on the dark web include black markets for selling weapons, drugs, forgeries, banking details, stolen goods and credit cards and new identities; illegal porn forums and file-sharing sites; political dissent and hate sites; and hacking communities.

Many people refer to the dark web as the Wild West of the internet, where anything goes. It is an online space where people have total freedom to buy, sell, share or create anything they want, confident that their activities can't be traced back to them. Some people want to buy murderous substances and implements. Some want to sell people and poisons. Others want to share livestreams of torture or create pictures and films of such depravity that seasoned cops who view them need counseling. And some people want to hire a hitman.

In 2016, there were at least a dozen sites on the dark web offering hitman services. The most popular and profitable murder-for-hire outfit was called Besa Mafia. Besa Mafia opened shop in December 2015 with a slick and professional site. Borrowing from the success of the darknet markets like Silk Road, Besa promised to match buyers and sellers of services. Someone could either sign up as a potential customer, or they could offer their services as a potential killer, hacker, thug or loan shark. When a customer posted a job, Besa would assign a nearby operative, holding the money in escrow until the job was done to the customer's satisfaction.

While some dark web hitman sites had tried to convey the impression they were the suave, shadowy figures depicted in books and films, Besa Mafia admitted outright that their hitmen were gang members and drug addicts— stupid, but willing to murder a stranger, provided they were paid. The advantage for the customer was that they never needed to meet the killer face-to-face, or even reveal their identity. They could pay for the hit in Bitcoin, a cryptocurrency that was the favored method of paying for illegal goods and services on the dark web.

On April 25, 2016, the Besa Mafia website was hacked, revealing an extensive database of names, addresses and photographs of people who had been targeted for murder. At least a dozen of these names had bitcoin addresses attached to them, meaning that the people placing the hits were serious enough that they had paid large sums of money.

The hacker released the database quietly onto the internet where it was picked up by cybersecurity expert Chris Monteiro, who in turn passed the information on to a trusted journalist, as well as to law enforcement. Chris came up against significant barriers trying to get crime agencies around the world to take the threat seriously. Tales of dark web hitmen and their unsuspecting targets, and of murders being organized over the shadowy dark web, sounded ludicrous. It was a full month before the FBI decided to look into the most unusual situation that had come to their attention. Many in the Bureau remained confused about what exactly they were investigating.

Although the hack did not provide any information about who was behind the site, or of the customers who placed orders—the dark web technology did its part to cover all traces—it did provide photographs and personal particulars of the people on whom hits had been requested. Among the files was Order Number 30312:

Target: Amy Allwine.

Description: About 5'6", looks about 200 lbs.

The order asked that the hit be taken out when Amy would be at La Quinta Inn, Moline Airport. She would be driving a dark green Toyota Sienna minivan. There was a link to a photograph that showed a happy Amy on a family holiday in Hawaii. The associated bitcoin address showed that bitcoin worth around $12–13,000 had been paid to Besa Mafia for her murder.

The person ordering the murder called themselves "Dogdaygod."

———

Dogdaygod first contacted Besa Mafia on February 15, 2016. The initial message said: "I am looking to hire you for a hit, but what is the recommended way to convert cash to bitcoin anonymously?" The site required payment in bitcoin, and Dogdaygod was concerned that pulling out a large sum of money to buy bitcoin would raise the suspicion of the authorities. Cryptocurrency was still a novel concept, and beginners usually made purchases via exchanges, which required proof of identity. Dogdaygod needed advice on how to hide the transaction.

The response from Besa Mafia was swift and helpful. The customer service administrator provided Dogdaygod with the names of a couple of bitcoin traders that did not require identification and suggested there were several ways to explain away the missing money, such as purchasing goods and services like training or consulting, or gambling online.

Dogdaygod wrote back: "The target will be traveling out of town to Moline, Illinois in March. What is the price in bitcoin for hit and ideally making it look like an accident?"

Several emails went back and forth between Dogdaygod and the administrator of the Besa Mafia murder-for-hire site. The starting point was $5,000, which would be a hit by a low-level gang member wearing a turtleneck and using a handgun. Staging an accident would usually cost an extra $4,000. They eventually settled on $6,000 for a gang member to wait at a predetermined location and ram Amy with a stolen car.

Dogdaygod was cautious and had many more queries about how the escrow system worked and what sort of guarantees Besa Mafia would provide to ensure the job was carried out. The hitman coordinator responded to each query politely and patiently. Eventually Dogdaygod was satisfied, saying: "OK, I did some research and everything that I read says that you are real and can carry out what you say you can do. They say that Besa means trust, so please do not break that. For reason that are too personal and would give away my identity I need this bitch dead, so please help me."

Dogdaygod submitted the order through the website's

online order form, along with a picture of Amy. The order
provided all of the pertinent details:

```
Amy Allwine
   She is about 5'6", she looks about
200lbs.
   Saturday   night   (March   19)   She
should  be  staying  at  La  Quinta  Inn
Moline  Airport  5450  27th  St,  Moline,
IL 61265
   Sunday  (March  20)  She  is  supposed
to  be  participating  in  a  Dog  trial  at
Quad  City  Christian  School  4000  11th
St, Moline, IL
   She  should  be  driving  a  dark  green
Toyota Sienna Minivan
   I  want  her  dead.  That  is  the  13  bit
coins,  if  it  can  look  like  an  accident
then you can have the rest.
   Not    sure    if    the    picture    is
downloading.  I  got  it  from  here:
http://www.allwine.net/travellog/hawaii/
```

In subsequent messages, Dogdaygod advised the
hitman that Amy would have a companion with her when
traveling to the dog training event from Minneapolis
through Cedar Rapids to Moline, but "no one that I care
about."

Besa Mafia agreed to take the job and told Dogdaygod:
"On March 19 make sure you are surrounded by people most
of the day, or in public places where they have video
surveillance. This way you ensure that no one can ask you
where have you been on March 19. If you have good alibi,

they can't do anything else than say it was accident and close the case."

Dogdaygod responded: "Thank you for the reminder. I will make sure I have a good alibi."

The transaction was completed, the bitcoin paid and everything set in train for Amy Allwine to be killed in Moline, Illinois on March 19.

On March 20, Dogdaygod wrote to Besa Mafia asking whether the job had been carried out, saying: "I have not seen anything, do you know if this is done?"

Besa Mafia replied: "No not yet. The hitman has followed her, but he did not have the chance to do the hit yet; he needs to be in a position where he can hit her car to the driver door, to make sure she dies." Besa Mafia suggested a sniper might be a better option than a hit and run, provided nobody would suspect Dogdaygod if Amy was obviously murdered.

Dogdaygod responded: "No, I would not be a suspect. I am fine with whatever you think is best."

Besa Mafia assured Dogdaygod that a sniper had 100% success rate, but would cost another $6,000. Dogdaygod did not have that sort of cash handy and the assigned hitman was apparently unable to find an opportune time to ram Amy's car, so the hit was not carried out.

The next day, Besa Mafia wrote: "We don't usually ask this, because we are not interested in the reason why the people are killed, but if she is your wife or some family member, we can do it in your city as well; making it look like accident or robbery."

Dogdaygod wrote back: "Not my wife, but I was thinking

the same thing. How much would it be to kill her at home, and then burn the house so that they cannot tell if anything was stolen or not (I am not sure if they have anything worth stealing)? This Thursday I know she will be home between about 9 and noon Central time. Her home address is 7624 110th St S, Cottage Grove, MN, 55016 (near Minneapolis)."

Besa Mafia agreed to kill Amy at home and burn down the house, but it would cost an extra ten bitcoin (around \$4,500 at the time). Dogdaygod deposited the extra funds the next day and promptly emailed Besa Mafia in a panic, that the deposit may have gone to the wrong bitcoin address: "HELP! wrong bitcoin address My screen refreshed and gave me the wrong bitcoin address where I sent the other funds. Are you able to match them up? It went to 1FUz1iECnhN2K-w8MUXhZWombbw1TCFVihb"

Bitcoin addresses are a string of thirty-four characters and numbers. Each address is unique and is proof that a transaction took place. There is a myth that bitcoin transactions are anonymous. On the contrary, anyone can go online to the site blockchain.info and see exactly when and how much bitcoin has moved into or out of an address. Every bitcoin transaction that has ever been made is recorded and is visible in this way. Where the anonymity comes in is that, without more information, it is impossible to tell who is on either side of the transaction, or what the transaction was for.

There are an almost infinite number of bitcoin addresses available. When someone is providing nefarious goods and services, the provider will often change the receiving bitcoin address for every purchase to make it more difficult for investigators to identify an address as relating to a particular business. When Dogdaygod deposited the second amount of bitcoin, Besa had provided a new address, but Dogdaygod had accidentally used the previous address.

The hitman reassured: "I have checked and the bitcoin has credited to your account."

With that out of the way, Dogdaygod got down to business. "OK, I got some more details on her schedule. I am trying to get as much as I can without being obvious. It looks like she will be home tomorrow from 12–1PM and Thursday from 12–1PM. Those are the only times that know about at the moment. Let me know the plan so I can be somewhere else public. I know her husband has a big tractor, so I suspect that he has gas cans in the garage, but I do not know that for sure. She usually drives the Sienna so if that is there she should be home."

Thursday, March 24 came and went, and Amy was not killed. Besa Mafia said the hitman had problems trying to get to the location and asked if the hit could be carried out another time. Dogdaygod replied: "Yes, I do want it done, but I have to pretend to be her friend to get this information and it's driving me crazy to be nice to her. I am also afraid that if I dig for information too many more times that it will look strange."

They rescheduled for the following Monday morning, but this time, according to Besa Mafia, the assigned hitman was stopped by the police for a registration check and, as he was in a stolen car, was taken in for questioning.

Dogdaygod was getting frustrated and wrote: "I realize that things happen, but this bitch has torn my family apart by sleeping with my husband (who then left me), and is stealing clients from my business. I have had to continue to act like her friend to get information and I cannot do it any more. I have gone out of my way to try and get you good information. I feel that I am at risk of being suspected if I ask too many more questions. You have had three good attempts at her and none of them have worked.

"I liked the idea of shooting and fire, because I think it would look like a robbery and cover up, but I am at the point that I do not care how it is done. I believe that if I go about my regular routine that I will not be a suspect, if I stop asking questions and just act normal.

"If it is not done in some way by May 1st then I would like my money back. Does that sound like enough time for you? I cannot get my hopes built up again like I did this weekend. I do not care about date or method, you have her picture and address, so you can tail her or do whatever you need to do to get the job done. I ask that you only get her and not the dad or kid as the kid is a friend of our child's and I do not want to leave him orphaned.

"I do know that she is going to take a trip to Atlanta the weekend of April 7 to 10, but I do not know the details. I also was passing by recently when they had the garage door open and I was able to see that they have three 5-gallon gas cans just outside the door from the house to the garage, and what looked like a propane tank as well. I am not sure if any of them are full, but they are there.

"Thanks for your help with this, I need her out of my life, so I can move on."

3

A NORMAL SUBURBAN HOUSEWIFE

As the story unfolded in the Cottage Grove Police Station, Stephen and Amy Allwine were in shock. As far as she was aware, Amy had no enemies. She never even had disagreements with anyone, personal or business. She was a normal suburban housewife who had just three things in life she cared about: her family, her church and her dogs. She was adamant that she had never been, and would never be, unfaithful to her husband. Their marriage was rock solid and infidelity would go against everything she, and her church, believed in.

Amy Allwine, née Amy Zutz, grew up dedicating herself to her faith and to helping others. Born to a couple who were adherents to a fundamentalist religion that later became known as the United Church of God, Amy was the middle child, with an older sister and younger brother. The children were not allowed to take part in extra-curricular activities at school, nor did they have any friends from outside the church. Amy attended Woodbury High School, where her participation in school life was limited to lessons. Nevertheless, Amy had a happy childhood and a social life

that revolved around the family's faith. She was an enthusi-
astic cheerleader for the church basketball team, and put a
lot of time into putting together dance routines for the girls
on the squad. Adhering to the conservative values of the
church, there were no skimpy outfits or suggestive moves in
Amy's choreography.

Amy met Stephen Allwine when they were both
students at Ambassador College in Big Sandy, Texas.
Stephen was also from a family that worshiped at the United
Church of God. Not so much an educational institution as a
training ground to prepare youth for life and service in
church, the college had the motto: *Recapturing True Values*.
The pair shared a love of dancing and got to know each
other through church socials, where they would always
choose each other as partners. After college, Stephen moved
to Amy's hometown of St Paul, Minnesota and they married
on August 11, 1996 in Cottage Grove. On that joyous occasion, Amy's father, Charles Zutz, placed Amy's hand into
Stephen's and said, "Take good care of my little girl."
Stephen swore he always would.

Both Stephen and Amy were deeply committed to the
church. God and religion played a central part in their life
together and they were determined that their future children would grow up observing the faith. The United Church
of God adheres strictly and literally to the teachings of the
Bible, including those of the Old Testament. In some circles,
the small religion, also known as Armstrongism, is defined
as a cult. Members are expected to marry only within of the
faith, which meant, according to one former member, "the
pool was very small."

Stephen and Amy did not observe Christmas or Easter,
in accordance with the church's teachings which regarded
both as pagan celebrations. The Allwines attended services

every Saturday at a modest building in St Paul. They would arrive around 12:30 p.m., a good hour before the service began, and would stay for all the activities afterwards, not leaving until the evening.

The couple spent most of their spare time together, and the bulk of that time was devoted to church business. They traveled a lot, serving congregations around the world and taking part in humanitarian efforts. The two were ordained as deacon and deaconess of the United Church of God in the spring of 2006, Stephen a month before Amy. A year later, they adopted their only child, a son. Amy brought him home when he was just two days old. It was an open adoption, and the Allwines stayed in touch with his birth mother. The birth mother chose them because Amy was unable to have children, and she liked that they were dog people and a very loving and affectionate couple. The desperately wanted child became part of the family and joined the tradition of Friday night dinners with Amy's parents and brother. On those nights, Amy's mother would put out the good china and silverware, while her father prepared the food. Amy always brought dessert, usually strawberry pie, which was her mother's favorite. When he was old enough, their son would join Amy in picking the biggest, juiciest fresh strawberries they could find to make that pie.

A friend of Amy's, Jane Sharpe, later told *48 Hours*, "When she talked about her son, her face changed, from happy to happier, if that's possible."

Well known and loved for her generosity, Amy traveled extensively doing charitable deeds and spreading the word of God to developing countries. The entire family—Amy's parents, siblings and husband and later their son—traveled overseas every other year for the Fall religious festival of their church, the harvest feast.

A my's primary passion outside the church was dogs. She had been a dog lover since childhood and, as an adult, she became an active and popular member of the dog training and competition scene. Before long, her Australian Shepherds were frequent competition winners, thanks to Amy's talent for training.

Her knack with dogs saw Amy turning her hobby into a career, training other people's dogs to compete in agility trials and competitions. She opened her training school, Active Dog Sports, and threw herself into the business of dog training in a way that was consistent with her values. Although her core business was to train dogs to be competitive, she did not put pressure on owners who attended the training just for fun. Her clients—both dog and human— adored her. The dog training shed on the property was three times the size of the house and Amy made sure it was kept immaculate. Active Dog Sports grew to be a respected and successful business offering an array of dog-related services and leading the way in dog nosework. Amy's sunny personality and her training by positive reinforcement saw her friendship group among fellow dog lovers grow to become second only to her church group.

Despite her growing success, Amy's first priority continued to be her family and her faith. She would never work or attend agility shows on Saturday, which was her Sabbath. Everyone who knew her confirmed she had just three things in her life: church, family and dogs. She excelled in all three. She was anointed deaconess of the local chapter of her church, she was a devoted and involved mother and wife, and her reputation as a pioneer in the dog training world, as well as her popularity among that scene, blossomed. She became a leader in the field of dog nose-work, traveling all over the country for competitions and trials, which were judged by the K9 division of the police departments.

Amy was known for being relentlessly positive, outgoing with a sunny disposition. Friends claimed she was never without a huge smile and they described her as a sweet, friendly and loving person. She was never negative, never judgmental and never gossipy.

While being utterly devoted to her faith, Amy was not evangelical to those who did not share her beliefs. According to those who knew her in the competitive dog circles, one of her most outstanding attributes was her empathy. Part of that empathy was her ability to imagine how she would feel if someone were to impose their beliefs onto her. Some of her more casual acquaintances later expressed surprise to discover her religious beliefs ran so deep.

Stephen was just as committed to his faith as Amy, but quieter than his exuberant wife. He was happy to let her shine in the spotlight, while he pursued more solitary and cerebral pursuits, or worked on turning the prefabricated house into their home. After becoming a deacon, he rose to become an elder, with responsibility for counseling couples, giving sermons at church and anointing those who fell ill.

According to the church teachings, "God, not man, established the marriage union at creation. By Him marriage exists, not only for now but forever. The word forever is used deliberately." Divorce could lead to excom-munication of a member, with the website stating: "Even if couples have a short courtship, fail to counsel before marrying or have dysfunctional backgrounds, none of these recognized troubles justify the later putting away of a mate with the freedom to remarry. Marriage is a commitment for life. Failure to plan properly is not grounds for the future dissolving of a marriage." With the ties of marriage taken so seriously, as part of being a church elder, Stephen provided premarital counseling for young couples, and advice and guidance for newlyweds.

Stephen and Amy organized social events and dances for the teens in the United Church of God. They maintained a website dedicated to the evaluation of popular songs. "We want to be confident that we are providing good music with good messages," the Allwines wrote on the webpage where they collated approved music for pastors and church elders to use for dances. "There is a lot of Christian music out there, but we also want people to realize that there is mainstream music that is OK to enjoy, as well." Any songs that implied sex outside of marriage, or spoke to the occult, suicide or drug use, would fail the test, as would songs that had videos with suggestive dancing. The couple posted videos of themselves teaching basic dance moves, showing an appropriate distance between partners.

If there was one thing Amy was perhaps not satisfied with, it was that she weighed more than she might have liked. She was constantly on one diet or another in an attempt to get it under control. She had hired a personal trainer to assist her. But she loved delicious food and, despite her abundance of energy, those extra few pounds stubbornly refused to go.

Jane Sharpe referred to her as "the salt of the earth" and told *48 Hours*, "She always was smiling, always smiling. You could look in her eyes and just see good."

Amy appeared to have it all. She seemed to be the last person in the world that should have been the subject of a dark web hit, but there was no question that the details provided to Besa Mafia were about her. It was her photograph, her home address, and she confirmed that she had been in Mobile when she was supposed to be the victim of a hit and run.

Under normal circumstances, what the FBI had uncovered represented a clear and present danger for Amy. Someone had paid between $11,000 and $13,000 to have her killed. The money was going to a sophisticated hitman network that employed thugs, snipers and gang members to carry out homicides. She should have been offered protection, with the case a top priority for law enforcement. Yet the previous day, the FBI had advised Stephen that Amy was not in any immediate danger.

They had good reason for this. The hacked data from the murder-for-hire website had revealed something else. Besa Mafia was nothing but a con, and Dogdaygod had been one of the worst scammed.

The scam was carried out in classic "Nigerian prince" style. The whole operation was likely owned and run by a single person, who called himself Yura. Anyone who provided bitcoin was strung along for as long as Yura could manage, upsold on services and fleeced of increasing amounts of money until they eventually gave up. In many ways it was the perfect racket. The people he was defrauding could hardly complain without implicating themselves in a serious felony.

A total of 147 messages went back and forth between Dogdaygod and Besa Mafia, with plans made to kill Amy Allwine on over a dozen different days. Yura wrote paragraphs placating Dogdaygod and sympathizing: "I am really sorry to hear what she did. Yes she is really a bitch and she deserve to die." Then he would ask for more money.

Finally on May 20, 2016, Dogdaygod gave up and

demanded a refund, writing: "That's it, your local guys suck. They cannot do simple things even when given plenty of time. I will try again later with one of your pros, but I will need to save up for that. Can you give me a quote of what I would need to work with a pro and then I will try to get a new order worked up in a couple months. Until then please refund my money."

Besa Mafia responded by telling Dogdaygod that the site had been hacked, and if Dogdaygod didn't cough up another ten bitcoins, their emails would be forwarded to the police. That was a little over a week before the FBI visited Cottage Grove.

It was a relief to know that there was not some shadowy hitman ready to strike at Amy when she least expected it. However, the fact that Dogdaygod had been scammed and Amy had never been in any danger from Besa Mafia did not change the fact that somebody who knew intimate details of Amy's life had paid a large sum of money to have her killed, and that they presumably still wanted her dead.

4

TAKING PRECAUTIONS

F BI Special Agent Asher Silkey asked the Allwines if any of the details in the messages made them think of anyone in their lives. Amy was adamant that she had not carried on an affair and that she could not imagine who Dogdaygod might be. The best lead they had was the assertion in one of the email messages that if Amy died, Dogdaygod would inherit her business. Amy's husband Stephen had no interest in dogs and knew nothing about the business of dog training. At Asher's urging, Amy and Stephen put together a shortlist of people Stephen would be likely to consider handing the business over to if anything happened too Amy.

Amy reluctantly provided the names of her colleagues, including her best friend, Sharon, and fellow dog trainers, Gayle and Kristin. Of all of them, Stephen and Amy said the clues pointed most closely to Kristin, who had helped Amy set up her computer network and online presence. Not all of the hints supplied by Dogdaygod added up, but Kristin watched the Allwine's dogs while they were away and her child sometimes played with the Allwine's son, just as the messages had said.

Interviews with Sharon, Gayle and Kristin went nowhere. All three women seemed genuinely confused by the questions put to them by police, which were designed to elicit information without revealing too much. With no other leads, the police asked Amy to provide a list of everybody who knew her well, especially in the dog training world. Amy provided hundreds of names and the FBI made some discreet enquiries of those who might have access to the level of detail about Amy's life that Dogdaygod had. The overwhelming response was that Amy did not have an enemy in the world and nobody could think of anyone that would do her harm. Amy appeared to be universally loved by everyone who knew her and every single person the police spoke to was adamant that there was no way Amy was having, or had ever had, an extramarital affair.

With their enquiries going nowhere, Special Agent Asher Silkey provided Amy with his business card and told her to contact him any time she wanted. He advised the Allwines to install extra security measures at their residence and report any suspicious activity to the police immediately. Stephen set about installing an alarm on the secluded house and put new codes on the garage door. He set up motion-detection cameras on each entry point to the house, other than the patio door that led to the backyard where the dogs usually roamed all day and would keep setting the cameras off unnecessarily.

The Allwines became more vigilant about their surroundings. In June 2016, Amy called the police to report a suspicious blue van parked at the end of the street. Police attended and startled awake a man who worked nearby and had slipped away for an afternoon nap at the entry to the peaceful Grey Cloud Dunes. It was perfectly innocent, but Amy was unsettled nevertheless.

Stephen decided on a more drastic measure. Although the Allwines already had a shotgun and two rifles, on June 22, 2016, he applied for a permit to purchase a handgun for personal protection. He and Amy went shopping and settled on a Springfield 9mm. They kept the gun in a handgun case under Amy's side of the bed, and the key inside a cupboard next to the bathtub in the ensuite bathroom. On their date nights, when their son was looked after by his grandparents, they skipped dinner and movies, instead going to the range to learn how to shoot properly. Amy also went out with her brother, a keen shooter, for some extra lessons. Stephen slept with the shotgun on his side of the bed. The handgun was locked in a small GunVault safe underneath Amy's side. Biometric programming meant that the safe would spring open at the touch of Amy's fingerprints.

Stephen also obtained a concealed carry permit for the 9mm, but rarely had cause to use it. He and Amy had a long discussion about whether, if someone came at him, he would be able to shoot them and Stephen didn't think he could. The one time he did carry the handgun was when he visited Kristin when she asked him over to help set up a wifi security system. The Allwines weren't sure who they could trust. The visit was without incident.

After the FBI's visit, Amy took Special Agent Asher Silkey at his word and started contacting him regularly. She let him know what was going on in her life and how she was feeling about it. The two struck up what Asher described as a friendship and had a number of telephone conversations and several meetings in person. Stephen attended at least two of these meetings, but sometimes Amy would meet with Asher alone.

Several weeks went by without incident. As often happens, Stephen and Amy became lax about setting the alarms on the doors. In particular, they didn't want the alarm accidentally going off when their son was around, as he was highly susceptible to loud noise and would become distressed. They resumed their day-to-day lives—Stephen working at his two jobs from the basement, Amy conducting dog training classes and both of them participating in church activities and looking after their son.

Although she confided in her best friend, Sharon, and the two of them puzzled over who could possibly be behind the plot, Amy kept the threats to herself. She didn't even tell her parents, for fear that they would worry. She downplayed the seriousness to people who knew about the threats after being questioned by the FBI. From the outside, nobody could tell anything was wrong. Amy continued to be bubbly and happy when she attended her regular meetings with the dog community. She still had a marriage that was the envy of many and fulfillment through her close family and her faith.

However, she would sometimes sit and talk with her sister and admit that, privately, she was devastated that there was someone that thought the world would be better off without her, and she had no idea who it was. It had broken Amy's heart to provide names of her friends to police. They were people she knew and loved and she did not think for a moment they had anything to do with threatening her life.

On July 31, 2016, Amy Allwine called Asher on his cell phone, clearly upset. She had received a disturbing email, she told him. When she told him what it said, Special Agent

Asher Silkey jumped into his car and went straight to the Allwines' house.

Amy had received an email from an anonymous email address from someone called Jane. It said:

```
Amy, your family is in danger. Last
Sunday you received an email with the
solution to this problem, and you have
not done anything about it yet. Are
you so selfish that you will put your
families lives at risk? If you did not
see the email then check your junk
mail soon.
```

Amy did not recall any such emails, so she checked her spam folder. Sure enough, there was an email from the same person, calling themselves Jane, dated a few days earlier. It said:

```
Amy, I still blame you for my life
falling apart. I do not know how a fat
bitch like you got to my husband, but
because of you he left, and my life
has become shit. I am sending you this
email, because it looks like you
already know about me. I see that you
have put up a security system now, and
I have been informed by people on the
Internet that the police were snooping
around my earlier emails. I have been
assured that the emails are
untraceable and they will not find me,
but I cannot attack you directly with
```

them watching. Here is what is going to happen. Since I cannot get to you, I will come after everything else that you love. I know about your son, your husband, and your business, and thanks to the internet (www.radaris.com) I see you have a mother and father in Woodbury, a brother in St. Paul, and a sister in Yardley, PA.

I have been busy researching topics on the internet, and have found that if you inject water into the brake line, then you will cause them to fail. What would happen if the brakes on the truck failed when your husband was hauling a heavy load? I found how to blow up a gas meter and make it look like an accident. I know that the meter on your house and on your business are on the east side, and the meter on your parents' house is on the south side. I am still watching you and your family. While, I did not see your son this week, I saw last friday he was wearing a bright pink shirt. I see that you moved the RV. Here is how you can save your family. Commit suicide. If you do not, then you will slowly see things taken away from you, and each time you will know that you could have stopped it, which will eat you apart from the inside. By the time

I am done you will want to end it
anyway, so why not do it now and save
them. Based on lasthope.com the best
ways to do it are shotgun to the head
(which you might not have) cyanide
(which you probably do not have)
gunshot to the head (which you might
not have) shotgun to the chest (which
you might not have) explosives (which
you probably do not have) hit by train
jump from height (a lot of bridges
around) hanging household toxins
(anti-freeze, ammonia and bleach)
inhaling gas (carbon monoxide)
slitting wrist or throat. I know about
this website, because I have thought
of this option many times. Remember if
you do not get it right the first
time, then you will likely be
committed for mental health issues,
and you will lose your business and
possibly your family. so I would pick
a reliable method. I think it is an
easy choice. 1 life to save 6 lives.
Your family does not need you, but you
can save them. DO NOT tell ANYONE
about this email or this deal is OFF
and I will come after your family. You
have seen that the police are not able
to track my earlier emails, but I was
informed of them searching. They will
not be able to track this either, but
I will know if they look into it.

> Unless you are a heartless, selfish
> bitch then I expect to see your
> obituary in the paper in the next
> couple weeks.

Amy was understandably upset by this new turn of events. Special Agent Asher Silkey asked Amy about the information specified in the email, and she confirmed that details such as the location of the meters and the fact her son had been wearing a pink shirt the week before were correct. However, the writer had been wrong about the address of her sister, who had long since moved.

The FBI took the threat seriously and asked Stephen Allwine for consent to review the family's electronics, which he gave immediately. The feds took away their computers for imaging—copying of all of their contents—and returned them a day or two later. The FBI found nothing helpful or relevant to the investigation on any of the family electronics.

The FBI also revisited some of the people involved in the dog training world and imaged their electronics as well. Again, they found nothing of significance to the case.

Through several email exchanges with the FBI, Amy was eventually placated by the suggestion to her that the move from trying to arrange for Amy's murder to trying to convince her to kill herself was an overall de-escalation of the situation. As to tracing where the email came from, thanks to the anonymity afforded by the dark web, there was little the FBI could do by way of linking an IP address to a real person.

Amy assured Special Agent Silkey that she would not be taking Jane's advice to kill herself. Her family needed her and it would have been at complete odds with the teachings of her church.

A few weeks later, she enrolled in the eight-week Cottage Grove Citizen's Police Academy. Under the question on her application asking why she was interested in attending the academy, Amy wrote: "I would like to learn more about the police department, what it does, and how it works. I would also like to see what I can do to support them better as a citizen."

When it came to the four-hour ride-along with an officer that was part of the experience, Amy naturally requested she be assigned to accompany an K9 officer.

In October 2016, the Allwine family, including Amy's husband, son, parents, brother and sister, went on their annual pilgrimage to the United Church of God's Fall Festival Feast in Germany. The whole family noted that Amy was happier and more relaxed than she had been in a long time, far away from Cottage Grove and the person who wanted her dead.

5

DEATH COMES TO COTTAGE GROVE

On the afternoon of November13, 2016, after a morning spent trap shooting, Troy Larsen was cleaning his koi pond when he glanced across the road. He had lived on 110th Street for eleven years and had met his neighbors, Stephen and Amy Allwine, but he didn't really know them. Today he noticed that heavy, white-gray smoke was coming from the Allwines' wood burner. He only noticed, because it was unseasonably warm—Troy was wearing just a T-shirt—and none of the other neighbors had their wood burners running that day. The dogs were barking, but then the dogs were always barking. Troy Larsen went back to tending to his pond.

That afternoon, several people were in the shed that housed Active Dog Sports training, a few yards away from the Allwines' house. Some of the trainers had independent access to the facility, which they could book online for private dog training sessions. Today there was a canine nose-work class that went from 4:45 p.m. to 5:45 p.m. that consisted of a trainer, Barbara, and five students. The students were startled some time toward the end of the class to hear screeching and skidding tires right outside the building, as if somebody was leaving in a hurry. It was odd enough that two of the students, Denise and Jennifer, exchanged looks that said, "What the hell was that?" It was not odd enough that anybody went outside to check. The class finished by 5:45 p.m. and everyone was gone by 6 p.m.

A little before 7 p.m. that evening, Stephen Allwine arrived home with his son, who went inside on his own as Stephen unpacked the car. As Stephen removed his shoes in the mud room, his son came back and asked, "Why is Mommy lying on the floor?"

Amy was beside the bed, staring up at the ceiling. She was warm, but there was no pulse, which was unsurprising given the blood and brain matter on the floor beneath her head. The gun was near her left elbow and one shell casing was near her right foot.

Stephen called 9-1-1. "I think ... I think my, I think my wife shot herself. There's blood all over," he said.

The operator tried to get information out of him as he spoke to his anxious son in the background. Stephen provided the address, as well as details on the number of guns in the house, as the operator guided him through the important points. He had last seen Amy, he said, when he left the house some time between 5:00 and 5:30 p.m. The operator asked him to check on his wife to determine if she was still breathing.

"She is not breathing. I, I can't tell where she's shot. I don't know," Stephen said, as his son sobbed in the background.

Cottage Grove Police Department patrol officers arrived while Stephen was still on the phone, standing in the garage with his son behind him. Beyond them, the smell of roasting pumpkin wafted from the kitchen. Amy was on the floor of her bedroom with a single bullet hole inside her right ear, a 9mm Springfield handgun on the floor beside her. She lay flat on her back, arms splayed out to the sides, in a pool of blood beside her neatly made bed. Her pants were undone and her red sweater was slightly pulled up, displaying her stomach and underwear.

Sergeant Gwen Martin, one of the first responders, was stunned to recognize Amy from the Citizen Police Academy. She had grown fond of Amy during the eight-week course where Gwen taught local citizens about law enforcement and emergency services. They'd last seen each other at graduation just two weeks earlier. On her class evaluation, Amy had written, "I would like to do this again in a few years." She was passionate about her business, eager to learn during the academy, and future-oriented. Nothing in her demeanor suggested she was suicidal.

Gwen broke down when notifying Detective Sergeant Randy McAlister, who was the on-call detective that evening. There was an apparent suicide, she told him, and he needed to attend.

Detective Sergeant Randy McAlister was bemused. Suicides, while tragic, were a common enough occurrence for the Cottage Grove Police Department, and not one that required a detective to attend. Gwen's manner also concerned him. The sergeant, who was also a trained paramedic, was abnormally distraught. As her voice choked, she handed the phone to her partner, Sergeant Pat Nickle. Pat told Randy that the victim had been a recent graduate from Gwen's class in the Citizen's Police Academy, Amy Allwine.

Randy felt the stirring of recognition at the name. "She was the one that was threatened on the internet that time," Pat filled in. The detective sergeant lost no time in getting dressed and making his way to the Allwine house. Once there, he was on the alert for anything that looked out of the ordinary. One of the first things he noticed was the smell of cooking pumpkin. It occurred to him that a woman planning on committing suicide was unlikely to be cooking dinner shortly before. There was also something not quite right with the blood beneath and around the body, and there was a film over the floorboards outside the bedroom as if they had been recently cleaned.

Examining the scene more closely, he noted that there was a large pool on the carpet around Amy's head, which was to be expected, but Randy was more interested in the drops to the left. He had seen many suicide scenes over the years, as both a paramedic and detective, and these looked out of place, as though they had dripped from something being suspended from above the area. What's more, blood from Amy's nose and mouth had dripped down the left side of her face, despite her being flat on her back. This suggested that at some time her head had been on its side and was later placed facing upwards.

The clean patch on the wooden floor just outside the bedroom door was at odds with the rest of the house, including the bedroom, which was messy with dog hair and didn't look like it had been cleaned for some time. Suicide was not a foregone conclusion in the matter of Amy Allwine.

A s the police secured the crime scene, Stephen stayed outside with his son. Officer Liermann joined him outside and quizzed him on the events of the day, preceding Amy's death.

Stephen told police he had been working from home that day as he usually did, from the basement. Their son was sleeping in, as they had all been to a church activity the evening before and he had gone to bed later than usual. Amy spent most of the morning clearing up the play area, but after breakfast she had told Stephen she wasn't feeling well. He checked on her a couple of times throughout the morning and allowed their son to play on the iPad so he wouldn't disturb her too much. All three of them had lunch together around midday, after which Amy went to lie down.

Amy's father, Charles, came to the house that afternoon to finish installing a new dog door that would allow Boson, the Newfoundland, into the garage when it was cold. Charles was a frequent visitor to the home and enjoyed helping them with handyman projects. He put Boson and George, the Australian shepherd, in their kennels in the mud room so that they would not disturb him doing the job.

Stephen told Charles that Amy was feeling poorly and lying down, so her father decided not to bother her. He finished the job, and left the house without speaking to his daughter. Five minutes later, Stephen called Charles, asking him to return and pick up his grandson, as Amy had decided to go to the hospital. Stephen had gone to check on her and she was flushed, her face looked bloated and her eyes were wide. Charles returned to pick up his grandson, who was waiting outside for him and took him home.

Stephen said that when he went back to Amy, she was sitting up and looked a little off. She said she was light-headed, dizzy with a dry mouth. She said some things that didn't make sense to him, as though she was remembering discussions they hadn't had or was seeing things that weren't there. Stephen googled the symptoms, which he found were consistent with a stroke or heart issues. Nevertheless, Amy changed her mind, deciding not to go to hospital, but to remain in bed while Stephen continued to work. She got severe migraines sometimes, especially when she had her period, and they had been more frequent since the incidents with the FBI. He said he looked in on her one more time, before he went to collect their son at around 5 p.m. She was kneeling beside the bed, and Stephen assumed that she was praying.

Usually either Stephen or Amy would take their son to his evening Ninja Warrior class, but Stephen stopped to get gas and then spoke to Charles about Amy's health for a while. By the time they got into the car, Stephen had decided it was too late to go to Ninja Warrior. Instead, the father and son went straight to dinner at Culver's, a fast food restaurant about a five-minute drive from their home. They texted Amy to see if she wanted them to bring her home anything. Stephen and his son ate in the restaurant while they waited for Amy's reply, but she never responded. Stephen offered up the receipts for both gas and dinner to the police.

When they got home, Stephen removed his shoes in the mudroom as usual. The dogs were still in their kennels, as Stephen had not released them after Charles had left earlier. When his son ran out to say that he had found his mother lying on the floor, Stephen checked on her, then called 9-1-1.

Police allowed Stephen to call whoever he needed to. His first call was to Amy's parents, Charles and Diane Zutz, to whom he blurted out, "Amy is dead. She shot herself." Charles and Diane rushed over, along with Amy's brother. Stephen also called their pastor, Brian Shaw, who dropped everything to come to the house. Stephen told officers that Amy had not acted or claimed to be depressed that day. In fact, she had been getting better lately, something that was corroborated by her father Charles. Stephen provided his two cell phones—a black Samsung Galaxy S7 and a silver iPhone 6—and their passcodes to police. He readily submitted to a test for gunshot residue on his hands, as well as allowing DNA samples to be taken from both him and his son.

When Amy's parents arrived, Officer Liermann clarified the times that Stephen had provided. Charles offered up his phone, which showed Stephen had called around 1:55 p.m. for them to come pick up his son, and again around 5:30 p.m. to arrange to collect him. Amy's parents said their daughter had given no indication that she was depressed or wanted to harm herself. Charles stated he could not believe she would have killed herself as he knew that her husband and son were the world to her. They were unaware of the vicious emails or the dark web threats that had been made against their daughter.

When Amy's parents advised the police that Amy was right-handed, which was inconsistent with the gun placement by her left elbow, that was enough for Detective Randy McAlister to want another set of eyes. He called the Minnesota Bureau of Criminal Apprehension and asked for one of its teams to attend the scene.

The rest of that night, the house was swarming with law enforcement officers from Cottage Grove Police Department and the Bureau of Criminal Apprehension. Some officers went door knocking among the neighbors to determine if they had noticed anything. One of the neighbors mentioned the screeching car that had left the street in a hurry earlier. Neighbors Roland and Linda Henley said they saw a pickup going past "real fast" Sunday night, just before 6 p.m. A car and a pickup right behind it, going real fast, so much so that they commented on what a hurry they were in

Law enforcement officers and the medical examiner stayed at the Allwine house until early the next morning. They sprayed luminol on the floor, which showed that a significant amount of blood had been spilled in the hallway, then tracked through the house at some stage. They bagged Amy's hands to preserve to test for gunshot residue and prepared her for autopsy.

6

INVESTIGATION OF A DARK WEB
MURDER PLOT

After all the formalities had been taken care of and Amy's body had been taken away by the medical examiner, the Cottage Grove police set to work. They had never had a case quite like this before and nearly everyone at the station got involved in some capacity.

One of the first things they did was go back to look through the files the FBI had created about the threats made to Amy through the dark web. One detective decided to do his own dark web exploring. He discovered that Dogdaygod had not limited his dark web expedition to the Besa Mafia murder-for-hire website. Somebody with the same username had created an account on the Dream marketplace after negotiations with Besa Mafia broke down. At the time, Dream was the leading large, eBay-like one-stop market where buyers could by any drug imaginable, as well as an array of other illicit goods. Like Besa Mafia, purchases were made with bitcoin and users transacted under a cloak of anonymity. Unlike Besa Mafia, it was a real market that sold genuine, though illegal, products.

Dogdaygod had made just two posts on Dream. The first

was in the Marketplace discussion forum where Dogdaygod wrote: "Looking for drug dealer physically located in Minneapolis area. Looking for a partner for a job, need to be willing to stay anonymous and be paid by bitcoin."

The second post Dogdaygod made said: "Does anyone have Scopolamine for sale?"

Scopolamine is a drug used to treat nausea and motion sickness, but it is dangerous in large doses. It is sometimes referred to as the "zombie drug" as it is said to induce amnesia when too much is ingested. It can make the user so drowsy that they are incapacitated, and it can make unsuspecting victims highly susceptible to suggestion. The drug is made into an odorless and tasteless powder that quickly dissolves in liquids, and it is commonly put into drinks or sprinkled on food. Victims become so docile that they have been known to help criminals rob their own homes and empty their own bank accounts, not even realizing that they are doing so.

In the United States, scopolamine is only prescribed via transdermal patch and is offered at a very small dose.

Although Dogdaygod didn't get a public response to the first request, there were two replies about the scopolamine. The first anticipated that it was to be used for no good and said: "There is a seller, but avoid that shit mate. It's dangerous as fuck and you WILL kill someone."

However, the second response provided Dogdaygod with the name of a seller of the drug: "Yeah bro try p3nd8s on Dream but be careful that shit will make you gladly hand over your kidneys and have no idea where why or who to when you come back to reality."

When Detective Sergeant Randy McAlister heard about this, he made a phone call to the medical examiner and made a request that the examiner had never received in the entirety of her career. Randy asked her to test Amy Allwine for the presence of scopolamine.

T hat was not the only odd thing that turned up in the early investigations. Upon reviewing the 9-1-1 call, something else stood out. As Stephen spoke to the operator and simultaneously spoke to his son while Amy lay in a pool of blood, the little boy asked his father quite clearly, "Are you gonna remarry?"

Stephen laughed and replied, "I don't know, bud."

The detectives decided it was time to interview Stephen Allwine again.

7

A CONFESSION

W hen detectives invited Stephen Allwine to attend the police station for a further chat two days after Amy's murder, he agreed immediately but brought two people with him—his attorney, Kevin DeVore, and the regional pastor for the Twin Cities, Little Falls and Duluth Minnesota congregations of the United Church of God. Pastor Brian Shaw oversaw the educational, social, and recreational programs of the congregations and provided counsel and guidance to local membership.

On this day, Pastor Shaw was asked to wait outside as Stephen and his attorney attended the interview with Special Agent Michelle Frascone of the Bureau of Criminal Apprehension. Stephen said he did not want anyone from the church hearing that Amy had killed herself, as suicide was against their beliefs. The church also held strong views on subjects such as infidelity and divorce. Anyone guilty of breaching the marital vows by either means would not be allowed to hold a formal position in the church and may even be asked to leave the congregation altogether.

Before inviting Stephen in that day, Special Agent Frascone had attended the Allwines' house at the request of Randy McAlister. She and her team had noted several things that were inconsistent with suicide. The purpose of her interrogation was to explore other possibilities and find out more about the contract that had been put out on Amy's life.

Stephen attended the station dressed casually in blue jeans, a gray T-shirt and a black jacket. He introduced himself as "Steve," took a seat at the table and leaned forward, his face resting on a clenched fist. He said that he was shocked when the FBI told them that someone had paid for a hit on Amy on the dark web. "We're a normal family," he said. "Nothing unique, nothing strange. The idea that somebody out of the blue would just want to kill somebody out of our family was just obscene."

He relayed the story of the threats that had been made online, and the emails that had been sent to Amy, apparently from the same person. "The email said if she didn't kill herself, they would come for her family. They had some details that indicated they were watching us." Although Amy was deeply distressed, Stephen did not believe she would actually do it, as anyone who committed suicide would not be allowed to enter Heaven.

Special Agent Frascone asked, "When she received these emails, was there a gut feeling of somebody you attributed these to?"

Stephen replied that some of the messages gave very specific information that pointed to a fellow dog trainer. "Kristin ... I've gone blank on her last name, I've always just called her Kristin." He said that some of the information seemed to fit, but other details were off. Significantly, the messages suggested the author was a single mother, while Kristin was married. He offered up that he had no idea where Amy's dog trials took her, but Kristin did, and she had made the arrangements for the Moline trip. The same information had been provided to Besa Mafia, and Amy had told Stephen she didn't know who else would have known those details. She hadn't known herself until a couple of days before leaving. Stephen told the investigators that he had taken a gun with him when he went to Kristin's house to assist her set up her network. "We still didn't know whether we could trust her, or what the deal was," he said.

Stephen said when he and Amy were discussing who he would be likely to hand over the business to if anything happened to her, the first person who came to mind was Amy's best friend, Sharon. "She's always been so helpful and I can't imagine her doing anything. Amy didn't either, but, you know, that was the first person who came to mind so we gave Asher her name." When Special Agent Asher Silkey questioned Sharon, he found nothing to suggest she had anything to do with the plot. The next name the Allwines gave him as someone who might take over the business was Kristin.

Stephen was subdued and softly spoken during the questioning, providing all the information requested with little emotion. When he talked about finding Amy, he broke down in tears. "If she did kill herself I didn't see anything comin'. I guess it was my fault," he sobbed. "I guess I don't even know what to look for, I don't know what..." He said that her routine had been a little different, and she'd been off her food the two days before.

Stephen's voice strengthened and became clearer when he spoke about his church. He confidently rattled off the history and rituals of the United Church of God when queried about the family's religion. At all other times he kept his head bowed, voice muted, usually hunched over the desk on his elbows.

He told police he couldn't explain the cleaned up blood on the hallway floor outside the bedroom and said nobody in the family had had any injuries as far as the know. He said he had not heard of the dark web until the FBI visited. He went on to say that it was frustrating for him because his work was in IT, and he had a hard time grasping the fact that the emails could not be traced. He said that the FBI had not allowed them to see the messages between Dogdaygod and Besa Mafia, but that Asher had told them what he thought they should know.

When he spoke of when he and Amy met, Stephen reminisced about college and the fact that she always seemed to be there when he needed a dance partner. They hung in the same social group and their relationship grew into a deep friendship before blossoming into something more. "I tell people, if you can, marry your best friend," he said.

When the police asked again about the allegations by Dogdaygod and "Jane" about Amy being a homewrecker, Stephen said emphatically, "She did not have an affair."

Then Stephen dropped a bombshell. It was not Amy who had been unfaithful. Stephen had a mistress. Her name was Michelle and she knew all about Amy.

Stephen and Michelle had met on a website called Ashley Madison. Ashley Madison was a dating website with a difference. Rather than matchmaking singles looking for love, it catered exclusively to those who were seeking an extramarital hookup. Not surprisingly, the site came under considerable criticism for its brazen advertising: *Life's short. Have an affair.*

Stephen claimed he had learned about Ashley Madison from younger church members during his counseling sessions. He logged on to the website out of curiosity. Once there, his curiosity got the better of him and he started online chatting, before deciding to meet with some of the women he was flirting with. His first attempt, dinner at the Legends Golf Club with a woman by the name of Autumn, was pleasant but awkward, though it ended in a kiss. When he got home, Stephen wrote: "Thanks for joining me this evening. I had a wonderful time. You are an interesting and beautiful woman. I would love to get together again some time. Thanks for the kiss. I would love to share more of those with you in the future."

Autumn responded: "Hi Steve. It's nice to hear from you. Honestly, I thought you were bored with meeting me and I'm surprised to hear that you felt otherwise."

Stephen replied: "No, Sorry. I was just really tired. I got back from Hong Kong last Friday and still getting over some of the jet lag. Since it sounded like you did want to head back to your place with your daughter there, I thought it was too late to plan something else. I figured it was best to call it a night. Would you be up for a second date sometime? Since you have been dancing before maybe meet at the caves for a Thursday night swim dance. Unless you know of something closer down that way." The two never had a second date.

His next match, Michelle, proved to be more successful. Michelle was a small, slim blonde in her forties who suffered from anxiety and depression. Michelle was married, but she claimed it was an open marriage as they no longer had a sexual relationship. Stephen and Michelle started seeing each other in October 2015, when Stephen offered to attend a doctor's appointment with her. After that they met for coffee, lunch, dinner and sex, most often when Amy was on one of her many trips attending dog training events and competitions.

Their trysts usually took place at Michelle's house, but Stephen also took her on two work trips. On the first getaway, their luggage did not arrive at the same airport as they did, which sent Michelle into an anxious spiral. Stephen took charge, arranging a hire care to go to where their luggage had been sent, then setting Michelle up in a charming B&B in Hartford while he worked. Her stress abated when she saw how calm and practical he was in the face of multiple problems, although the lost luggage stressed her out enough that she rarely left the B&B.

Their second extended trip was to Syracuse, again when Stephen had to travel for business. This time Michelle felt more comfortable and roamed the town while Stephen worked. She met him back at the hotel in the bar for Happy Hour when his day finished. There they enjoyed a few drinks, sometimes taking selfies on Michelle's phone of themselves laughing or kissing.

As an anxious, nervous person, Michelle appreciated Stephen's kindness and polite demeanor. He sometimes spoke of Amy, saying he didn't know what the future held for their marriage. He told Michelle that Amy didn't spend enough time with the family, preferring to be working with the dogs and being part of the canine community, from which Stephen felt excluded. He never spoke of his faith, so Michelle was surprised when she googled him and discovered that he held a position as a preacher in the United Church of God. His photograph and links to sermons were on their website, alongside articles that laid out the teachings of the church, including those that said infidelity was a sin and that a member of the United Church of God could never divorce.

Around February 2016, Stephen told Michelle that he and Amy had been up late doing their taxes and had had a long talk about their marriage. Stephen and Michelle's relationship started to cool off. Nevertheless, they still met up from time to time. They met for lunch on Stephen's birthday in March, but he was running late because he had locked his keys in the trunk of his car. In April, Stephen finally gave in to Michelle's curiosity about where he lived. Amy was out of town at another dog show, and Stephen walked Michelle through the house. April was the last time they were intimate together.

A few months later, in September 2016, Stephen and Michelle met for lunch. Stephen told Michelle about the FBI visit and the threats against Amy. He told her that the threats were coming from someone who hoped to take over the business. Michelle responded, "Who would want to kill somebody over a $50,000 business?"

S tephen told the police about Michelle in his interview that day, but he referred to it as a short fling that happened a couple of years earlier. He said it started as a friendship and that Michelle was going through a rough time in her life. As he was a minister, he played more of a counseling role. He said he had told her about the FBI investigation because it was a stressful time in his life and he needed to share it with someone.

Stephen decided there was no need to tell his pastor. He also decided Amy's parents did not need to know, especially as Stephen and his son were in the process of moving in with them. Amy's parents had insisted that they could not possibly stay where the tragedy had occurred.

Shortly after the police interview, Stephen moved in with his grieving in-laws, keeping them completely in the dark about his extramarital affair.

A SUSPECT

Investigators tracked down Michelle and made arrangements to interview her. In the meantime, police also revisited Amy's colleague Kristin. She had been in Oklahoma at a dog show on the day of Amy's death, something easily verified by police. She stated that, since the first time detectives had questioned her, she had wanted to take Amy aside and speak to her about the threats on her life, but the time and place were never quite right. She found it hard to believe that either Stephen or Amy would ever be involved in any sort of extramarital affairs and when the detective asked her directly, she denied ever having had any sort of intimate relationship with Stephen. She described the couple as very loving, and said that Amy very much cared for Stephen, as he did for Amy.

The message Dogdaygod had sent to Besa Mafia said that Amy would have a companion while she was traveling to Moline, where she was supposed to come to an untimely end. Dogdaygod told the hitman that Amy's companion was not someone they cared about. Kristin was the person who traveled with Amy that day. It would be strange indeed for

Kristin to put herself in potential harm's way like that, and it was strong evidence that Kristin was not Dogdaygod.

Another twist hit the investigation when the test for scopolamine in Amy Allwine's system came back positive for an amount that was forty times the therapeutic dose for motion sickness. Such a level would cause blurred vision, confusion, and hallucinations, with the victim being receptive to doing anything someone demanded of them. Suicide was all but ruled out, and Randy McAlister assigned a team to investigate the death of Amy Allwine, which the police department was now definitely treating as homicide.

Murders were rare enough in Cottage Grove, but murder for hire was unheard of. Terms like "dark web" and "bitcoin" were unfamiliar to the Cottage Grove Police Department before the Amy Allwine case. However, there had been one police report, lodged and then forgotten about, way back in March. It popped up when the police did a search for potentially related cases.

Someone had walked into the Cottage Grove Police Department in March 2016 and made a very unusual report. They had been defrauded in a bitcoin transaction. The person said they had entered into a transaction with an individual known only as Mark, to purchase training and test preparation materials for $6000. Mark wanted to be paid in bitcoin, which was acquired and transferred, but the goods were never received. The complainant's suspicion that they had been defrauded was aroused when they noticed that "Mark" had used an untraceable guerrillamail address in his email of March 3, 2016 confirming the transaction. The materials were never received, and the complainant filed a report with Cottage Grove police marked "theft by swindle."

Cottage Grove police were not familiar with bitcoin and didn't really know what was being reported to them. In any event, the person making the report didn't seem too concerned about the police following up on the crime. The police took the report and filed it away without any further investigation.

But now a bitcoin transaction report in early March 2016, the same time Dogdaygod was paying Besa Mafia to murder Amy Allwine, seemed very significant indeed. Detective McAlister pulled out the paperwork to see if it held any clues.

The complainant who made the report was Stephen Allwine.

Now that the police had a reason to look at Stephen more closely, they became even more thorough in their searches. Five officers were assigned to almost full-time hours uncovering and sifting through the evidence. The police seized all the devices they could find belonging to Stephen and Amy Allwine, including computers, laptops, phones and hard drives. Detective Sergeant Randy McAlister provided a total of sixty-six electronic devices and media to a private computer forensic service for forensic analysis.

There were thousands of emails and pages of data for law enforcement and the independent computer forensics investigator to sift through, with little hope that anything could be recovered. Stephen Allwine was an IT specialist. If he was guilty, he would have covered his tracks. However, the specialists were able to recover some evidence from Stephen's MacBook Pro that had not been completely obliterated.

Stephen had told police that he had not heard of the

dark web prior to being contacted by the FBI. However, before the hit was placed on Amy, his MacBook was used to search for the Tor network, which is the software required to get onto the dark web, and an operating system called TAILS, which eradicates all evidence of Tor-based activity from the computer it is on. A user called "sallwine" used Stephen's MacBook to conduct Google searches for installing the TAILS operating system on an Acer computer. Notably, no Acer-branded computer or device was found by, nor provided to the police.

Shortly after Dogdaygod sent the first message to Besa Mafia, Stephen's MacBook was used to conduct searches for MoneyGram and Bitcoin. The user "sallwine" made several more searches for bitcoin, as well as visits to a bitcoin exchange, over the next couple of days.

Just minutes before Dogdaygod sent a message to Besa Mafia describing exactly where Amy would be in Moline, IL, the user "sallwine" on the MacBook googled "K9 Nosework" and reviewed an online event calendar for the trials, then used Google Maps to calculate Moline's distance from Chicago. This was the precise information that was provided to Besa Mafia.

The photograph of Amy in Hawaii that Dogdaygod had provided a link for was uploaded to the family's public website just moments before Dogdaygod provided it to Besa Mafia. Shortly prior to the upload, "sallwine" had been browsing Amy's Facebook photographs, which were set to private.

On February 17, Stephen's MacBook was used to look up a $700,000 life insurance policy on Amy Allwine. The beneficiary was her husband.

The user "sallwine" conducted several searches for individuals on Radaris, a sort of White Pages, just days before

Amy received the threatening message that had details of her family, complete with an old address for her sister, that the writer, Jane, claimed had come from Radaris.

Not only did the computer forensics discover what was on Stephen Allwine's MacBook Pro, they made a note of what was *not* found, namely any evidence of the mysterious Mark, who had supposedly transacted with Stephen over email to sell training equipment for bitcoin, other than the single untraceable email supplied by Stephen to the police when making the claim. There were no other emails that would be expected when making a $6,000 business transaction. The message was sent using a guerillamail address, which is a service that allows anonymous sending of emails. Forensics proved that Stephen's MacBook Pro had been used to access guerillamail at that time.

Also found were emails between Stephen and woman named Rita, who was offering escort services on the website backpage.com. The emails appeared to be price negotiations for a night of sex, which was at odds with Stephen's insistence that his affair with Michelle was a one-off that began by accident.

All of this, along with other minor artifacts left on his computer and his phone, such as access to reddit and bitcoin exchanges, was mounting circumstantial evidence against Stephen Allwine, but nothing that could not be explained away by a clever lawyer.

Investigators started going painstakingly through backups, searching for deleted items or anomalies, until they came to a backup of Stephen's iPhone created on August 3, 2016. Within that backup was a Note that contained a single line of nonsensical letters and numbers. The note had been made, and then deleted less than a minute later, but not before it had been backed up to the cloud.

The single line of the note read: "1FUz1iECnhN2Kw8-MUXhZWombbw1TCFVihb."

The thirty-four characters and letters were identical to the address that Dogdaygod told Besa Mafia they had deposited bitcoin to as payment for carrying out the hit. The records showed the note was created around 20 seconds before the message was sent to Besa Mafia. Someone using Stephen Allwine's iPhone had copied the address and pasted it into the email to the murder-for-hire site.

Investigators had their smoking gun. Bitcoin addresses are unique, so this was a direct connection between Dogdaygod and Stephen Allwine's iPhone.

Other evidence started coming in. Stephen worked for two companies, and he said he had been working from his basement all day on the day that Amy was murdered. However, both companies confirmed that he had not logged onto their systems after lunch and he performed no work functions that afternoon.

A review of the Allwines' video doorbell system determined that no one had rung the doorbell that day until the police arrived, nor had it been turned off. The home security system data confirmed that nobody had come to the house from the time Stephen left until he returned, but somebody had opened the garage door three times during the time he claimed to be working in the basement. If a disgruntled dog owner had entered the house, they had somehow managed to avoid all monitored entry points, or had subsequently erased all traces of themselves.

When detectives interviewed Michelle, she confirmed that she had had an affair with Stephen after meeting him through Ashley Madison. She also told them about the day Stephen had been running late for their date in March, after locking his keys in his car in a Wendy's Restaurant carpark.

He had told her he had been there to meet a man to purchase bitcoin.

The circumstantial evidence was mounting and it all pointed to just one person—Amy Allwine's husband, Stephen, who was currently living in her parents' home with the little boy who had preceded his father into the house to find the corpse of his mother.

9

AN ARREST

On Tuesday, January 17, 2017, Detective Sergeant Randy McAlister briefed two patrol officers to arrest Stephen Carl Allwine for the murder of his wife, Amy Allwine.

Cottage Grove detectives set up surveillance across the road from Amy's parents' house, where Stephen was living. They saw Stephen's vehicle leave with him behind the wheel, but they could not tell if his son was also in the car. The officers followed him for a short distance and, as he turned southbound on Ideal Avenue, the squad car activated its emergency lights and made Stephen pull over. One officer withdrew his gun from its holster and demanded Stephen get out of his car. He obeyed meekly when they told him to put his hands behind his back and offered no resistance when they handcuffed him. A search of Stephen's vehicle turned up miscellaneous clothing, sunglasses, chargers and CDs, several dog collars, including a dog shock collar, an iPad, two computers and a Galaxy S7 phone.

Stephen was taken to the Cottage Grove Police Department, where he exercised his right not to talk to police without an attorney present, and was then transferred to Washington County Jail.

Despite the investigation having already taken two months, Stephen was charged with second-degree murder, which suggested a non-premeditated killing. This was surprising, given that Stephen had apparently been planning his wife's death for nearly a year.

Stephen soon posted the $500,000 bail, which had several conditions attached, including GPS monitoring and no unsupervised contact with his son. The child was to continue living with his maternal grandparents and Stephen returned to the house he had shared with Amy.

It was a matter of just two weeks before Stephen was arrested again, after Amy's parents reported to authorities that Stephen had tried to contact his son and had asked Amy's parents to charge up the boy's smart watch so he could track his movements.

The judge raised the amount required for conditional bail to $600,000 and ordered Stephen to have no contact with his son or Amy's parents. He once again managed to post bail and was free to return home.

On March 24, 2017, a grand jury elevated the charge against Stephen Allwine to first-degree murder. The judge set unconditional bail at $2 million and conditional bail at $1 million. This time, Stephen was unable to post bail, and he was remanded in prison to await trial.

10

TRIAL

S tephen spent almost a year in prison before his trial began. On January 23, 2018, after six days of questioning fifty potential jurors, the opposing attorneys finally settled on a pool of eight women and seven men to decide whether Stephen Allwine had killed his wife. Those who were chosen professed a working knowledge of computers, but no in-depth technical expertise. Three of them would hear all the evidence but be dismissed before deliberations. They would only be needed if any of the other jurors could not continue due to illness or discharge from their duty.

In his final case before retirement, District Judge B. William Ekstrum presided over the most bizarre trial Washington County had ever seen. Over the next week, prosecutors Fred Fink and Jamie Kreuser drew together the threads of evidence that pointed to Stephen Allwine being the Besa Mafia customer Dogdaygod, and the man who ultimately fired the bullet that took Amy Allwine's life.

The prosecution said that Stephen Allwine gave Amy scopolamine in her lunch, then got their son out of the house before shooting Amy while she was disorientated from the drug. He then cleaned up the blood and burned the cleaning cloth and any clothes that had been spattered in the incinerator. Later, he went to collect his son, carefully keeping receipts from the places he visited as an alibi, and then let the child go in ahead of him to find his mother in a pool of blood on the floor of the bedroom.

Stephen Allwine's motive for killing his wife was simply that he wanted out of their marriage. However, nothing was more important to him than his status in the United Church of God, and he would lose his role if he were to initiate divorce proceedings. In fact, the church would probably ask him to leave the congregation altogether.

In rebuttal, Stephen's defense lawyer, Kevin deVore, said: "All they have are theories, assumptions and facts. What they don't have: no fingerprints, no DNA, no confessions, no eyewitnesses."

Throughout the trial, the courtroom was filled to capacity with family from both sides, church congregation members and people from the professional dog training community. They took notes, which they would compare during breaks and probe for inconsistencies in testimony. Stephen and Amy's pastor would spend the breaks counseling family and friends who were trying to make sense of what had happened.

Stephen showed almost no emotion throughout the trial. He did not turn to look at his family and rarely acknowledged his own lawyer. Instead, he made a show of reading through every report and piece of evidence that was tendered and occasionally poured himself a cup of water. Sometimes, when it seemed appropriate (such as when the 9-1-1 call was played or when photographs of Amy's body were displayed), he would appear to be sobbing; however, the box of tissues in front of him remained untouched.

This most unusual trial called for a most unusual array of witnesses, including an escort, a bitcoin trader, Stephen's mistress, a pawnbroker, neighbors, dog trainers and an array of forensic and medical specialists, as well as the law enforcement officers who had attended the incident and worked on the case afterwards. The prosecution elicited responses from witnesses that cumulatively built an airtight case against the defendant. The bitcoin trader confirmed that he had met a man at a Wendy's fast food restaurant to sell him bitcoin, and Stephen's presence there was confirmed by his call to roadside assistance when he locked his keys in the car. The escort confirmed she had met Stephen through backpage.com, and that they had sex together at a cost of $400 for an overnight stay, long before his Ashley Madison flings. Several pages of email messages confirming these arrangement were put into evidence.

The bloody footprints matched Stephen Allwine's socked feet. The gunshot residue test was positive on his right hand, although the amount was minuscule and could have been transferred by contact with Amy. The furnace had been going that afternoon, despite it being unseasonably warm, which suggested someone had burned evidence. This also made it more difficult to pinpoint the time of death, as the excessive heat could have sped up decomposition. The security system showed there were no trips of the front door, garage service door, or egress window after Stephen Allwine left the house to pick up his son, meaning nobody entered the residence through any of those three entry points.

The prosecution's case ended with a detailed timeline of the improbable coincidences between the actions of Dogdaygod and the actions of Stephen Allwine. It was impossible not to draw the conclusion that they were one and the same.

Kevin deVore, did his best with what he had in Stephen's defence. There was a neighbor who may or may not have seen Amy around 5:00 p.m., when the prosecution said she was already dead. There were the reports from neighbors and the dog trainers using Amy's facility that two cars had roared away from the property at around 5:45 p.m. that evening. There was the unlocked, unmonitored patio door that was never tested for prints, and the dogs that were usually in the backyard to deter anyone from entering the house that way had been locked in their kennels. The prosecution said Amy had been killed in the hallway and moved to the bedroom; however, there was no blood on the carpet between the hallway and Amy, nor had the carpet in that area been cleaned. Slightly built and weighing just 240 pounds, it is unlikely that Stephen could have carried her there, and dragging her body would most certainly have resulted in blood stains from one area to the other.

With medical evidence ruling out suicide, the only alternative theory was that somebody else had killed Amy that evening. The intruders could have entered through the unlocked patio door, the dogs safely locked in their kennels, killed the scopolamine-dosed Amy while Stephen was at the gas station and the restaurant, and then roared off in two vehicles. However, with the overwhelming computer forensic evidence that fingered Stephen as Dogdaygod, all this theory did was suggest he had finally been successful in finding his hitman.

Just over two weeks after they had been called in for duty, it took the jury just eight hours to declare Stephen Allwine guilty of the premeditated murder of his wife, Amy. They accepted that, having failed to hire a hitman, he had pulled the trigger himself and then tried to cover up the crime.

At the sentencing hearing, Amy's family spoke of the hole in their lives. Her parents had come to the trial with open hearts, hoping that Stephen would be proven innocent. They had no clue about his infidelities, which went against everything their church believed in. They could not help but be convinced by the overwhelming evidence provided by the prosecution and the witnesses who took the stand. Amy's parents had provided Stephen with a home from the time of Amy's death until he was arrested, so they felt doubly betrayed when the evidence convinced them they had been housing not only an adulterer, but their daughter's murderer. In a statement read to the court on their behalf, they called Stephen selfish and said "forgiveness will take time."

For the first time, Stephen spoke. In a rambling speech that went too long, he maintained his innocence and love for Amy. He tried to explain an error that one of the experts had made when talking about bitcoin. He also said he had been housed in prison with drug addicts, child molesters and kidnappers, but that he was bringing God to them. Three atheists had been turned so far and were now attending bible studies regularly. "I've never asked for anything, except to work for God," he said.

Judge Ekstrum was having none of it. Addressing Stephen directly, he told him he believed he was a hypocrite and a "great actor," a cold and calculating killer who could "turn tears on and off." Stephen was sentenced to a mandatory life in prison without parole.

The United Church of God set about obliterating any mention of Stephen and Amy Allwine from their website, even going so far as to ensure that Stephen's bio and sermons were removed from the archives, unable to be dug up by even the most diligent investigators. The church put out a lengthy public release that expressed concern about the potential negative media coverage the case could bring the church given "the fact that Mr. Allwine was technically a lay (unpaid) minister at the time."

It barely mentioned Amy.

BESA MAFIA

B esa Mafia, the darknet website that Stephen turned to when he decided he wanted out of his marriage, continued to operate. Its owner, Yura, was unable to be located, thanks to the technology that underpins the dark web. Yura rebranded the business several times, giving it names like Crimebay, Chechen Mob, and 18th Street Gang among a myriad of others. Although the names changed, the modus operandi remained the same throughout each incarnation. Yura continued to receive a steady string of people hoping to hire a hitman, and they were fleeced to the tune of hundreds of thousands of dollars.

After Amy's murder, law enforcement in the United States and around the world began to take the information that came from infiltrations of Yura's sites more seriously. There were several more arrests of people who had paid Yura in the hope of having a hit taken out. Tina Jones, a nurse from Des Plaines, paid $12,000 in bitcoin to hire a hitman to kill the wife of her lover. She was sentenced to twelve years. Californian Beau Evan Brigham hired a hitman to murder his stepmother and received a sentence of three years.

In early 2020, Yura claimed to have retired, saying scamming would-be murderers was taking a toll on their mental health and it was time to open a restaurant. A new incarnation of Yura's website still exists on the dark web, however, although Yura claims to have sold the business.

It wouldn't be the first time Yura lied. But Yura did seem to have genuine remorse about the fate of Amy.

"I feel really sorry for that wife," Yura wrote in one conversation. "[the FBI] saw the messages about dogdaygod. Why didn't they do anything?"

FOR MORE ON THIS STORY

There is more to this story: For another perspective on the Amy Allwine case, as well as other cases arising from the hack of the Besa Mafia murder-for-hire site, plus extensive interviews with Yura, see The Darkest Web by Eileen Ormsby, published by Allen & Unwin.

The appendix at the back of this book includes:

- Transcript of the 9-1-1 call made by Stephen Allwine

- Transcripts of the emails from Stephen Allwine to "Rita's Playhouse"

- Unedited transcripts of all emails between "dogdaygod" and Besa Mafia

PART III

THE KIDNAP OF CHLOE AYLING

1

A CHILLING EMAIL

On July 12, 2017, London modeling agent Phil Green checked his emails. Phil's inbox was often filled with requests for models that fulfilled some criteria or the other for jobs that ranged from photo shoots and commercials to attending functions and parties to add a bit of glamour to the occasion. The business he owned was called Supermodel Agency, but none of the household names we would consider to be supermodels were on his books. The women represented by Phil were catalog models, promo girls, Instagram influencers and glamour models, or what used to be referred to as "Page 3 girls." Back in the day, British tabloid newspapers like *The Sun* and *The Daily Star* featured a topless woman on page 3, ensuring a boost in sales to people who probably weren't that interested in world events or local news. Phil's models adorned calendars on mechanics' walls and the pages of lads' magazines like *FHM*, *Maxim*, *Loaded*, *Nuts* and *Zoo Weekly*. The luckiest ones appeared in *Playboy*. Some of the models worked at lap dancing clubs to supplement their income, while others turned to webcamming.

Few modeling requests were off limits for Phil and he sent girls off to fetish shoots, jelly wrestling competitions where they would roll around in a variety of slimy substances, and jobs of public flashing, where a photographer just "happened" to capture an exposed boob or evidence of no knickers in a supermarket, on the side of a freeway, or in a crowded park.

Phil loved being surrounded by beautiful young women half his age. Whenever he went down to London from his home in Lincolnshire, he would arrange a party at one of the hot new nightclubs. In return for a supplying bevy of models to hang around and impress the punters, Phil and the girls would be treated to free drinks all night in the VIP area. He took every opportunity to schmooze with the famous, drop names and earn some cash, including putting his models in touch with tabloid newspapers like *News of the World* if they managed to hook up with a celebrity or sports star. The tabloids would pay big money for a salacious story, especially if it came with compromising photographs. Marriages and reputations were ruined, but the models got career-building exposure.

Scantily clad models attended trade shows or motor races as "hostesses," with ready smiles and a friendly demeanor that suggested the man they were talking to stood a chance of taking them home. The girls with the most Instagram followers might even be asked to audition for a role on TV as a game show hostess, or to appear in a reality TV series. Those at the top of tree were invited to compete on *Love Island* or *Celebrity Big Brother*.

On July 12, there was the usual array of emails seeking girls with this look or that, for one job or another. But there was one email that was very different. The email sender was the Black Death group and, as Phil read the message, a chill went through him.

The email claimed that the Black Death group had kidnapped one of Phil's models, who was on an assignment in Milan. She was being held captive somewhere in Europe. If Phil did not come up with €300,000, Chloe Ayling would be auctioned as a sex slave on the dark web the very next Sunday.

2

A JOB IN FRANCE

Chloe Ayling had joined Supermodel Agency one year earlier, in August 2016, when she was just nineteen years old. Although beautiful, at just 5'3", Chloe had no chance of becoming a fashion model. However, her ample curves and lack of inhibitions meant she quickly became a highly in-demand glamour and commercial model. She was soon one of the agency's most popular girls, with her wavy blonde hair that hung halfway down her back, impressive cleavage, slender waist, and hourglass curves. Chloe had an Instagram feed full of saucy photos that featured her in a variety of risqué poses wearing very little, if anything at all, often in public. Sometimes she was pictured with a girlfriend, giggling in a bubble bath or enjoying a hug that hinted they got up to a lot more when the cameras were turned away.

Before joining Phil's agency, Chloe had a legion of teenage boy fans, having been featured in strip football YouTube videos, where her job was to awkwardly kick a soccer ball in her high heels to a male teammate, who would then kick toward goal. If he missed, Chloe would remove a piece of clothing until she was standing as naked as YouTube would allow in the middle of a football field. She also had parts in prank videos where she stripped down to skimpy underwear in staged practical jokes. She didn't earn much for these videos, but believed they would raise her profile and lead to better jobs.

After she signed onto Phil's Supermodel agency, Chloe worked constantly, eventually earning £400 to £500 for a single magazine shoot. She soon became a popular choice for the *Daily Star*, the last newspaper to still feature Page 3 girls. Her star was rising, and so was the number of people, mostly horny guys, who followed her on social media.

It was no surprise to Phil when Chloe was specifically requested for a shoot in Paris for a motorbike magazine in March 2017. She was just the type of girl that motorcycle enthusiasts wanted to see straddling a new bike in a skimpy outfit. The email came from a photographer called Andre Lazio. Andre assured Phil that Chloe's expenses, including flights, accommodation in Paris, and spending money, would all be paid up front.

Part of an agent's job is to check whether the jobs and people the models would be meeting were legitimate. In his book, *Confessions of a Model Agent*, Phil Green said: "I checked his address, and this was perfectly legitimate, even to the point of looking at Google maps to find the location. I asked Andre Lazio to send me pictures of previous work he had done to which he duly obliged. He even sent me a picture of his studio, and there above the studio door were the words 'Bellismafique – a little Italian Temper in the heart of France,' exactly as he said."

This was enough for Phil to feel satisfied that it would be perfectly safe to send nineteen-year-old Chloe to France for the job.

Chloe was walking her beagle, Nylah, when she received the call from Phil telling her about the job in Paris. She squealed in excitement. This was exactly what she had signed up for—travel, glamour and adventure. Chloe had never been to Paris and she was itching to explore all the famous landmarks.

Phil told Chloe that the photographer wanted her exact measurements for the custom-made motorcycle leathers, so she had to be measured again, even though he had already taken them when she first joined the agency. Phil was known as "the man with the tape measure." He insisted on measuring all models himself, as he claimed to have been duped in the past by models who added inches to their chests and shaved them from their waists. Chloe reluctantly agreed to make the trip to Supermodel Agency's office, because she didn't want to miss out on the Paris job.

The shoot called for an overnight stay at the Hotel Madeleine Plaza, and Chloe requested the earliest flight possible to Paris and the latest one to leave, so she would have plenty of time to do sightseeing. The arrangements made by the photographer were detailed and thoughtful. The hotel didn't have a spa service, so he added an extra €150 to Chloe's expenses so she could enjoy a facial or a massage. He warned her not to wander too far late at night. Vigilant about all aspects of her safety, he assured Chloe and Phil that the motorbike arranged for the shoot had been fixed to the floor, so there was no chance it would topple as she shifted her pose for the photographs.

Chloe couldn't wait for the trip. She arrived in Paris on the morning of Thursday, April 20, a little thrill running through her as she spotted the driver waiting at the gate, holding a sign with her name in big black letters, ready to take her to her hotel.

The Hotel Madeleine Plaza was four-star accommodation in an area famous for its luxury boutiques and delicatessens. Her small room would have cost at least a couple of hundred euro. Chloe marveled that she had been specifically requested for this job, meaning she must have made quite the impression on the photographer.

Once checked in, Chloe wasted no time depositing her bags and heading out to see what Paris had to offer. She had one goal in mind: to see the Eiffel Tower. She walked the two miles to France's most famous landmark, calling Phil on FaceTime on the way so she could show him the sights. When she arrived, she took a selfie beneath the tower before walking back to have dinner on her own at a restaurant near her hotel. She ate quite late in the evening, as is the European custom.

Upon arriving back at the hotel, any plans for an early night were ruined by the sudden screech of a dozen sirens. Confused and worried, Chloe did what many nineteen-year-old girls would do—she called her mother. Her mother immediately panicked, having already been concerned about her daughter going to Paris alone to meet a strange man. Things didn't get much better when Chloe received a message from a friend of a headline that had popped up online: *Terror hits Paris as policeman shot on the Champs-Elysées.*

As Chloe bunkered down in her room, talking to her mother and then Phil, news began to filter through. Around the time Chloe had been having dinner, a man had roamed the Champs-Élysées shopping boulevard less than a mile away, wielding an AK-47 assault rifle, the weapon of choice for mass shootings. One police officer was killed, and two others, as well as a German tourist, were seriously injured. The gunman was shot dead and found to be carrying a note praising ISIS, along with addresses of police stations he had planned to attack. It was decreed a terror attack.

Although people in the immediate area were evacuated, Chloe was told to stay in her hotel room. The next morning, her breakfast was interrupted by a hotel employee with a telephone. The man on the other end of the line introduced himself as Andre Lazio, and told her that his studio had been looted during the attack. The thieves had taken off with all of his camera equipment and lighting gear. The shoot was canceled and he was sending a car to take Chloe back to the airport.

A little frustrated, but understanding that there was not much that could be done, Chloe finished her breakfast and checked out of the hotel, jumping into the car waiting out the front. It was only when she arrived at the airport that she realized she had taken the wrong car. The driver was demanding cash, but Chloe didn't have any, as she had been expecting to be handed her expenses later that day.

Chloe's first instinct was to call Phil to fix it, but she knew that was futile, not least because he was a late riser and wouldn't be out of bed. Instead she scrolled through her phone until she found the email with Andre's number on it. She called him, passing the phone to the driver so the two of them could figure it out.

After a conversation in French, which Chloe didn't speak, the driver made her understand she was to wait until Andre arrived with the cash. Chloe waited impatiently until a man finally appeared at the window.

Andre Lazio was very young to be such a senior photographer. He was probably not even thirty years old, and had cropped dark hair, an olive complexion, and a serious expression. He paid the driver and apologized profusely to Chloe, both for canceling the shoot and for the mix-up with the car. Andre seemed agitated and keen to get going. He gave Chloe the promised expenses and left her to wait several hours before her scheduled flight home, which was running late due to the terrorist threat. She spent the time updating her social media.

Although she didn't get to the shoot, the trip wasn't a complete write-off. Chloe had her expenses, and back in London she received plenty of publicity from the tabloids she modeled for. Never afraid of bending the truth to sell papers, the *Daily Star* wrote of the terror experienced by one of their top Page 3 models who was caught up in the drama as she walked along the Champs-Elysées when the incident unfolded. Naturally they accompanied the story with a picture of a topless Chloe.

Andre Lazio called Phil and told him that he and Chloe could keep the fee, but that he had decided to return to Italy as Paris had become too dangerous. He still wanted to work with Chloe however, and he would arrange another shoot later in the year, this time in Milan.

3

A JOB IN MILAN

A few months later, Chloe and her friend Danielle were on assignment in Dubai, which meant partying with the client, attending nightclubs and parties, and frolicking on the beach. When Chloe took a call from Phil, Danielle scowled. She didn't like Phil and often asked Chloe to leave Supermodel Agency and join hers. Chloe laughed Danielle's concerns off and told her she was happy where she was.

She was particularly happy after taking this call. Andre Lazio had finally decided to reschedule the motorcycle shoot. This time, the shoot would be taking place in Milan in early July, just a couple of weeks after Chloe's twentieth birthday. Chloe had never been to Milan. She was excited that she would be visiting a new city, one which many people considered the fashion capital of the world. Again, she requested the earliest possible arrival flight.

For his part, Phil once again checked the location of the studio on Google Maps, which convinced him the photographer and studio were genuine. Andre told him that he had booked a makeup artist and stylist to attend the shoot and get Chloe ready. She had been booked into the Best Western Plus on the Piazza Lima. Along with access to the gym and swimming pool, Andre had arranged complimentary spa treatments and breakfast.

Chloe couldn't be more excited. On the morning of her flight, she set her alarm hours earlier than necessary, just to be sure there was no way she would miss the plane to one of the most exciting modeling jobs of her career.

The next morning, awaking early in her luxurious hotel room in Milan, Chloe put on the outfit she had chosen for meeting the photographer: a pink chenille bodysuit, snug designer jeans, sneakers, a leather jacket, and a cap. She packed her suitcase, including the new bikinis she had bought the night before for her upcoming trip to Ibiza, where she was going to get a bunch of beach photos for her Instagram account. Always determined to be prompt to her photo shoots, she had checked out by 8:30 a.m. and was on the way to the studio, a twenty-minute drive away. After a day's shooting, she would be back on a plane home in time to debrief with her mother.

───────

L ater that night, back home in Surrey, England, Chloe's mother, Beata Ayling, was worried. It was nearly midnight, and Chloe's plane had been due to land at Gatwick Airport at 9:30 p.m. Chloe should have arrived home already. If the flight had been delayed, Chloe would have called. She always rang to let her mother know what her plans were and if they had changed.

Beata called Phil Green to ask if he had heard from her.

He had not, which was also a surprise, as Chloe usually called to let him know how a shoot had gone. Phil checked the flight and confirmed it had landed on time. Knowing that Chloe was booked to fly to Ibiza the next day, Phil suggested that she may have decided to stay in Milan another day and fly out directly from there. What young model wouldn't want an extra day in the fashion capital of the world? Beata had a hard time believing her daughter would make such a radical change without notifying her, but perhaps she had lost her phone. She reluctantly agreed when Phil suggested they wait until the morning and make enquiries if neither of them had heard from Chloe by then.

Beata did not sleep well that night. She was back on the phone to Phil first thing in the morning. He called the airline, who confirmed they had no record of Chloe checking in. She had disappeared.

With Beata hassling him to find out what happened to her daughter, Phil turned to his computer, wondering if an answer lay in his emails. Perhaps Andre Lazio had sent through some revised plans for the shoot. As he scanned his inbox, a sender name caught his eye: Black Death group. Curious, Phil clicked on it.

"Hi Phil Green. I go by the name MD. I am a mid-high level contract killer working for Black Death Group. Chloe has been taken and is currently under my wings and as long as I live nothing will happen to her, I give my word." The email went on to say that Chloe would be auctioned as a sex slave on the dark web the following Sunday unless Phil could raise funds from three men Chloe had named, two of whom Phil recognized as clients and the other, Rory, whom he did not know.

The email said that MD was protecting Chloe and that

he was risking his life by writing to Phil. However, he could not release her as "the sentence for that would be death for both myself and Chloe as a part of a rule that no merchandise leaves Black Death unpaid."

Phil responded to the email with a single word: "Received."

4

BLACK DEATH GROUP

B lack Death was a shadowy Eastern European organization that dealt in weapons, drugs, bombings, assassinations, provision of mercenaries, new identity creation and human trafficking. It also operated online auctions for sex slaves on the dark web.

A July 2015 article in *Motherboard* magazine detailed journalist Joseph Cox's encounter with the Black Death group:

"Nicole's starting bid is set at 150,000$," the listing read. The girl, skinny, blonde, and topless, appeared to be thrashing around in the accompanying photos. With her arms tied behind her back, and the rope connected to a wire frame, "Nicole" lurched forward as the shadow of a man loomed in the background.

The advert for the upcoming auction included Nicole's breast size, weight, and that she is free from sexually transmitted diseases. She was being showcased on the dark web, on a site run by a group calling itself "Black Death."

Joseph Cox attempted to infiltrate the site by pretending to be a bitcoin-rich potential customer, but he was not successful in gaining an audience at an auction and, possibly suspicious, Black Death terminated contact with him.

A year later, in May 2016, UK authorities were alerted to an online auction of two teenaged girls being held on the dark web. Fifteen-year-old Laura had a starting price of $750,000 and the website declared that the auction was "fully booked." Seventeen-year-old Gemma commanded a starting bid of $120,000.

Unlike most of the darknet market sites, Black Death did not advertise to the masses, and it changed URL addresses often, when the site got too much fresh traffic. Anyone who managed to find the site on the dark web was greeted by a drawing of figures wearing long robes and plague doctor masks, the type worn in the time of the original Black Death —the Plague. The mask features a nose that is half a foot long and resembles a black beak. During the Plague, the beak was filled with pleasant-smelling plants and spices to prevent the stench of rotting corpses getting into the wearer's nose. Nowadays, the mask is a common sight at masquerade balls.

The auction page of the site claimed that all girls, which the site referred to as "merchandise," were auctioned in Europe, but could be delivered to the winning bidder wherever they were in the world. The site also claimed the group could kidnap a specific target to fulfill the needs of customers, at a significant price. Black Death had a doctor on staff who would test the girls for sexually transmitted diseases and virginity, with girls declared "pure" commanding a higher price.

Only people who were personally recommended by current members could gain access to the auctions, with links being provided to those who expressed interest in specific girls. The next auction was six days away and Chloe Ayling was due to be sold then.

D espite the email telling him not to contact law enforcement, Phil called the police in Milan, but he found it difficult to make himself understood. They wanted him to come into the station to make a missing person's report, which was not very practical. He went on to call the British Consulate office in Milan, who were significantly more helpful.

Beata contacted the local metropolitan police in the meantime and they in turn called Phil. He provided them with the details in the email, including the names of the three men he had been told to contact. The police took over his email account so that they could liaise with the Black Death group under Phil's name without the group knowing they were really talking to police. The negotiations for Chloe's life were beginning.

Meanwhile, having been briefed by the consulate, the police in Milan were now taking Chloe's disappearance very seriously. A squad car was dispatched to the address of the studio where Chloe was supposed to be straddling a bike in motorcycle leathers. Officers discovered an empty building with a bit of builder's mess and temporary walls that created a makeshift corridor from the front door to the back of the building. In the corridor they found a suitcase that had been dumped just inside the door. Further into the building, they discovered a cell phone, jeans, shoes, and a pink leather jacket that had been hastily discarded. Next to the clothes was a piece of paper with a picture of eleven men in long gowns and masquerade masks.

Across the picture were scrawled the words "Black Death Group—Chloe." There was nothing in the building to suggest it had ever been used as a photographer's studio.

It didn't take long to ascertain that the suitcase and the discarded clothes belonged to Chloe. Police in Milan and the UK worked together to try and figure out what happened to the young model and where she might be being held. They had little to go on, but a team of investigators started the arduous task of trawling through CCTV footage in the area to see if they could piece together what had happened a couple of days earlier.

The police had taken over Phil's email to negotiate with the Black Death group. Phil was kept in the dark about what the police were saying, but it was evident that they had not offered to pay the money the kidnappers were demanding. Two more emails came through to Phil's account over the next couple of days from the mysterious MD, whose frustration was evident. One said: "I think I haven't been clear enough. My superiors tell me there is a high interest in Chloe for auction... Time is running out, auction is on Sunday. I might be a contract killer but real life isn't fucking John Wick. I will be unable to protect her if you people do nothing about it."

Another email sent through the advertisement that MD claimed was already on the Black Death website and being circulated on the dark web. It featured photographs of Chloe, apparently unconscious, in her pink bodysuit with the piece of paper they had found in the fake studio propped on her stomach. They were serious, and if Phil didn't come up with the money, a terrible fate was awaiting Chloe.

As the Sunday that Chloe was to be auctioned rolled around, Phil and the police waited with trepidation. Phil had managed only to extract an offer of £20,000 from one of the men on Chloe's list and the police in both Milan and the UK were mostly keeping him in the dark.

The police in Milan had been busy, but kidnappings were rare in Italy and apparently they had no further leads. They had sent Chloe's photograph out to all the police stations all over Europe, and were feeding back information about the investigation to the British police through Interpol. The deadline approached and they heard nothing. They had not been able to find the invitation-only dark website where the auction was to take place.

As the deadline passed, nobody was sure what the next steps should be. Nobody expected what happened next.

5

KIDNAPPED

On the Monday morning following the auction, as the British Consulate in Milan opened its doors at 9:30 a.m., a man and a woman walked in. Some consulate staff might have noticed the young couple enjoying a casual, leisurely breakfast at the nearby cafe earlier, laughing and chatting without a care in the world.

When the door opened, the two walked in together. The young woman was dressed casually, wearing a tracksuit that was too big for her petite frame. Upon approaching the counter, she told the receptionist she did not have an appointment, but it was an emergency and that she needed to be seen immediately.

The couple was ushered through the metal detector, past two armed soldiers, into the office of the consulate. Staff member Nicoletta greeted them and the blonde woman said, "I was kidnapped. I'm Chloe Ayling."

The staff at the consulate knew her name, of course. She was on the missing person's list and was subject to the highest alert in Europe, as it was suspected she was a victim of human trafficking. Her mother and agent had been calling constantly. Nicoletta immediately ushered Chloe into a private room and the man, who Chloe said was a friend, tried to follow. He was told to stay where he was, and a group of armed security surrounded him to make sure he did just that.

Chloe was sat down and questioned while the police were called. They asked who the man with her was and she told them he was a friend she had called when the kidnappers released her. But when the police arrived and asked her what number she called, she couldn't tell them.

Caught in this obvious fabrication, Chloe panicked. She told them that she might be free, but she had not escaped the clutches of Black Death. Then an extraordinary story came tumbling out of Chloe, a tale she told over several hours.

On the day of the supposed shoot, the taxi pulled up in a quiet neighborhood outside a peach-colored six-story corner building that looked mostly residential, although there was a pizzeria behind the shuttered door on the corner. The windows on the lower floor were covered in bars. There was no sign to suggest there was a studio inside, but a prominent number 7 to the right of the glass doors indicated that Chloe was in the right place. Beyond the glass doors was a staircase leading up. However, when she tried the doors, they wouldn't budge. A panel of buzzers to the left of the door provided no clues about which one she should press for the studio.

Chloe flicked through the emails on her phone until she found the number she had for Andre. She called it and the man who answered introduced himself as Daniel and directed Chloe a little way down the road to a smaller building, which looked more like a disused shopfront in a garage. He stayed on the line until she had located it. Chloe hung up the call and pushed the door open.

Modeling studios come in a variety of guises. Empty shops and unrenovated warehouses are particularly popular because of the versatility of large spaces and the ability to light the shot from all angles. Andre had described the shoot in detail in his email to Phil. The motorbike couldn't be bolted to the floor this time, unfortunately, but would be tied down with straps that could be photoshopped out later. There would be a green screen behind Chloe, so that scenery could be added later. Chloe had been to many shoots in a wide variety of locations, and nothing about this location set off any alarm bells for her.

Chloe dumped her suitcase inside the door and walked down a makeshift corridor toward the back of the small building until she found a wooden door marked "Studio." The sign featured white lettering on a black background and appeared to be stuck in a very temporary fashion to the door. She figured that must be the right room and inside would be the motorbike, cameras and lights, but she was unnerved by the silence. It was eerily quiet. Typically, a modeling shoot was a hive of activity, with loud music playing and the hustle and bustle of the dozen or so people usually needed to make a shoot happen.

Chloe was reaching out to open the door when she felt a gloved hand slam over her mouth and another snake around her neck. The assailant came from behind. He must have been waiting in the part of the shopfront that was blocked off from the entrance. As he held Chloe's head back so that she couldn't move the rest of her body, another man appeared in front of her.

This man was straight out of any young woman's nightmares. Cold, dead eyes glared at her through the eyeholes of a black ski mask, pale lips visible through the mouth hole, and, worst of all, he was brandishing a syringe.

Chloe's attempts at squirming away were ineffective against the much stronger men and there was no way of stopping the masked man from pushing up the sleeve of her pink leather jacket and sliding the needle into her right wrist. The last thing Chloe felt was her muscles begin to relax before everything went black.

6

CAPTIVE

Chloe awoke in pitch darkness with her wrists handcuffed together, her feet bound, and tape across her mouth. Groggy from whatever drug had been injected into her, and having trouble breathing through her nose, she tried to figure out what was happening. She could feel movement, but she was completely confined inside something. She felt hot and her heart was beating too fast.

Her first priority was to get the tape off her mouth. As she had been placed in the fetal position, she was able to raise her hands and pick the tape from her lips. The longed-for easy breathing didn't come, however, and she was only able to take short, shallow breaths. It was then it dawned on her that she had been stuffed into a bag that had been zipped up. She could feel the bag surrounding her bare skin, which also meant that at least some of her clothes had been removed after she blacked out.

Wiggling her finger against the zip, she was able to create a small gap that allowed some air in, which Chloe gulped gratefully. As the fog in her brain started to clear, she realized that she was in the trunk of a moving car. She was still wearing her bodysuit and socks, but everything else was gone.

Still not thinking straight, Chloe began to scream, calling for the driver to stop the car. She worked the zip of the bag until she could get her handcuffed hands out and hit them against the underside of the parcel shelf until it came tumbling down on top of her.

Her plan succeeded in getting the attention of the people in the car. She felt it swerve and heard doors opening, then the lid of the trunk open. But any hope she had that this meant she would be saved was dashed when saw two men looking down at her, wearing the same black ski masks. People with good intentions don't usually wear ski masks when there's no snow around. Wordlessly, they replaced the tape on her mouth and zipped up the bag.

The journey in the trunk of the car went on for what felt like hours. Occasionally her silent, masked captors would stop and open the trunk, check on Chloe and let her take sips of water. Each time they stopped, they replaced the tape on Chloe's mouth. Each time, she managed to remove it, even when they undid her handcuffs and re-cuffed her hands behind her back. She used her tongue to work the tape free, the sweat on her face ensuring that it didn't stick too fast.

When the car stopped a third time, a man climbed into the trunk with her, spooning her in the small space. She noted that the man was not wearing a ski mask, which did not bode well. If he was going to let her see his face, did that mean she was not expected to get out alive to identify him?

The man told her that the two men who kidnapped her

were Romanians who had now passed her on to him and the driver of the car. He murmured to Chloe in soothing tones that he had no plans to harm her. He answered all her questions, about where they were going, who was driving and why they had taken her with the same response: "I don't know." If his job was to reassure her, it wasn't working.

Helplessness washed over Chloe and for the first time she started to cry. Bound, but thankfully no longer gagged, she continued on her journey to a mysterious destination, the strange man spooning her in the trunk of a small car. Chloe had no idea what was in store for her.

When the car finally stopped, Chloe didn't know how long she had been in the trunk with her captor. He had tried to calm her nerves and Chloe was somewhat comforted by his soft voice and gentle manner. He had even gently pulled her bodysuit straight when one breast escaped, without any unnecessary touching. Whatever they had in store for her, it seemed rape was not on the agenda.

The two men pulled the oversized duffel bag around her and zipped it up, warning her if she struggled she would be injected with the sedative again. Nothing terrified Chloe more than the thought of the syringe, and she lay still so they could carry her. Chloe didn't weigh much, but she could hear the men breathing deeply as they carried her up what felt like a steep hill. She heard a door unlocking and they placed her gently down and unzipped the bag.

When her eyes adjusted, Chloe could make out a cluttered and messy kitchen and two men. The man who had been in the trunk with her had not bothered to put his balaclava back on, but the other man remained masked, silent and staring. Chloe asked meekly if she could go to the toilet and she was directed up bare concrete stairs that had a wall on one side but no banister. Her captor followed her to the door of the shabby bathroom, which he directed her not to close as she took care of her needs.

Next, the men led her through a beaded curtain to another small upstairs room. A chest of drawers took up the length of most of one yellow-green wall. A sleeping bag was laid down on the floor next to the chest, and there was a single bed on the other side, with a multicolored blanket made up of dozens of crocheted hexagons pulled neatly across it. The masked man pointed at the sleeping bag, indicating Chloe should lie on it. The men handcuffed her hands to one leg of the dresser and her feet to the other. Satisfied that Chloe wasn't going anywhere, her captors went downstairs, and she could hear them speaking in a foreign language.

After a while, the man who had been in the trunk with her returned. Still speaking in his quiet, soothing voice, he told Chloe that he had to leave now, but his boss was on the way to see her. Chloe desperately wanted him to stay because she was afraid of the silent masked man, but he told her gently but firmly that his job was done and he would have to tape her mouth again. Something was wrong, he told her, and the boss was angry. The masked man would wait for the boss, who would tell Chloe what was going on.

Chloe lay on the floor, unable to sleep, her movement limited due to the position she had been handcuffed in. Eventually she heard a commotion downstairs, men yelling and a door slamming, then an angry, one-sided conversation, apparently on a telephone. She realized this must be the boss and she wondered when he would come upstairs.

She didn't have to wait long. The man came upstairs and released the handcuffs around her wrist, leaving the ones around her ankles. He sat on the single bed, the only other piece of furniture in the room, and she twisted around so she could see him. What she saw made her mouth drop.

7

A STRANGE KIND OF PRISON

The man who sat above Chloe, the boss the other men were so afraid of, was Andre Lazio, the photographer she had met briefly in Paris. It dawned on Chloe that she had been lured to Milan specifically to be kidnapped. But why?

Chloe stared at the man on the bed. It didn't take long for the man to confirm that his real name was not Andre Lazio and he definitely was not a photographer. He told her she could call him MD. The men who had grabbed her at the fake studio, and the ones who had driven her to this house, worked for the same organization as him. The organization was called Black Death.

MD explained calmly to Chloe that he was one of the Black Death group's most highly ranked officers. Then dropped the bombshell. "You have already been advertised for sale," he said. "Your auction is supposed to be on Sunday."

To prove it, he showed her the advertisement on his laptop. Chloe looked in horror at a photograph of herself she had never seen before. She was lying on her back, wearing her pink velvet bodysuit. Although her eyes were open, they were glazed and staring into the distance, pupils dilated as though she were completely out of it. Her long blonde hair was splayed out messily around her pale face, as though someone had tangled it on purpose. A piece of paper was laid on her stomach, upon which was printed "Black Death Group—Chloe." It was a far cry from the carefully orchestrated and posed photographs in heavy makeup that peppered Chloe's Instagram. She realized the Romanians must have taken it after they had injected her and partially stripped her. She had no recollection of it being taken.

Next to the photo was a description that read:

> Chloe
> Born in UK
> Abducted in Italy
> Held in Germany
> 19 years old
> Caucasion
> 34DD-25—35
> Beginner model
> Starting bid €300,000
> Auction takes place 16/7/2017

The ad also linked to her Instagram account, so potential buyers could see what she looked like when she wasn't drugged.

Chloe was reeling. She realized the measurements were the ones provided by Phil so the photographer could custom-make her leathers for the photoshoot. They weren't for clothes, they were for the advertisement. MD told her that she had been stripped as soon as she had been drugged, to make sure she didn't have a tracking device on her. They had also checked her hair for hidden electronics. Chloe couldn't reconcile what she was hearing with the man who sat on the bed. MD was young and clean-shaven, not unattractive, and softly spoken with a gentle accent. He seemed kind. He did not look like a monster, yet he was a senior member of an organization that kidnapped and sold girls and young women.

MD wasn't finished. There was a problem he told her, and his superiors were not happy. She should never have been taken. He scrolled through the website to the list of rules that governed Black Death's auctions and pointed to one line in particular:

We do not sell girls that are terminally ill, pregnant, have STDs or are young mothers.

Chloe Ayling had a two-year-old son. Under Black Death's own rules, she could not be sold.

———

Chloe had fallen pregnant at the age of seventeen, when she was at college studying sports science. She had long since split with the father of her son. When her modeling career took off, the little boy split his time between Chloe and her mom, and living with his dad, leaving Chloe free to pursue her dream of becoming an international model.

MD went on to tell Chloe that her being lured to Milan and kidnapped was a complete mistake. The trip to Paris had been for the purpose of being taken and sold at auction, but when MD had checked her Instagram page and seen photos of her with her son, he had canceled the kidnapping. However, the men who carried out the snatchings had misunderstood, and had emailed Phil using the Andre alias to rebook her in Milan. That was what all the yelling and commotion downstairs had been about. MD had to answer to his own superiors. Chloe had already been advertised, and there was a lot of interest in her auction from some very powerful men in the Middle East. The Black Death group did not want to upset their wealthy clients.

MD went into more detail about what happened to girls captured and auctioned by Black Death. The younger the girl, the more he would be paid. Verified virgins commanded the highest prices. When the wealthy men bought a girl, they used her as a sex slave, passed her around to other men in their family, and then fed her to pet tigers when they grew bored with her. The tentacles of Black Death reached all over Europe and beyond. There were agents everywhere. It was, he told her, the largest Mafia-style organization in the world, with a hierarchy of twenty levels. MD was at Level 12 and he operated as an assassin for the organization, usually killing people by poisoning. The other men involved in her abduction were just lowly foot soldiers.

Chloe was understandably distraught but MD reassured her that he was going to do everything he could to help her. The Black Death group was first and foremost a business. If they could get the €300,000 that they had put down as a starting bid on Chloe, she would be allowed to go.

Chloe's head spun. There was just her and her mother, and no extended family who could provide that sort of money. She had only just started in her modeling career, and didn't have any savings at all. She had no close friends who had that sort of money either.

MD told her she needed to come up with the names of three people who would be willing and able to come up with the sum Black Death required to secure her release. Chloe provided the names of three older men: one she had been seeing, although they had had a falling out and weren't talking when she left for Milan; one who did PR for *Sixty6* magazine; and the owner of *Loaded* magazine. MD said he would email the names to Phil Green and tell him he had until Saturday to get the money together, otherwise Chloe would be put up for auction on Sunday, even though she had a child. She would be less valuable, but there would still be interest from men who wanted to carry out heinous acts on her.

C hloe spent her first night in captivity lying on the floor on top of the sleeping bag, still cuffed by both wrists and ankles to the chest of drawers. MD had brought in a red blanket that helped a little with the cold, but even if she could sleep, it seemed MD liked to chat. He came in and out of the room to talk to her, his presence announced by the rattle of the beads that formed the curtain in the doorway. He sat on the single bed beside her and rambled on about Black Death, his important role in the organization and the risks he was willing to take to help her. He said he would even pay part of the release money himself, provided she was able to raise the bulk of it.

Although she remained bound to the chest of drawers, she no longer had the tape across her mouth. MD told her she was at a property he owned and that they had left Italy while she was in the trunk of the car. It was remote enough that nobody would hear her scream anyway. He reassured her that she was not going to be harmed and certainly not raped. The penalty for any of Black Death's operatives who messed with the merchandise was death.

MD brought her food, usually pizza, but as he had mentioned that he carried out assassinations for the Black Death group by poisoning his victims, Chloe decided it was best not to eat any of it.

As the second day wore on, Chloe asked whether he had heard back from Phil. She was not at all impressed to hear that he had responded with a single word and nothing else since. She had no way of knowing the police had taken over his account.

That afternoon, as Chloe returned to her spot on the floor after a toilet break, MD said, "You can have half of the bed if you want to." The next room was a bedroom with a double bed. He told her that the farmhouse was so remote that she had no chance of escaping and, if she tried, she would be hunted down and killed. He took pains to let her know that it wasn't him that would hand down the death penalty, but the Black Death group, who had operatives everywhere.

Given the choice between the bed or going back to being handcuffed on the floor, especially knowing that Black Death would kill MD if he did anything that would "spoil the merchandise," it was an easy decision for Chloe to make. Although she was terrified of Black Death and what they might do to her, she was no longer afraid of MD. She believed him when he said he wanted to help her get away from the organization's clutches. She gratefully accepted his offer and that night they slept back-to-back, him under a yellow blanket and her under the red blanket he had given her earlier.

From then on, Chloe spent all of her time lying on the bed, other than when she wanted to go to the bathroom. MD had been very clear that she was not to go down the stairs or try to look through the shuttered windows. He told her about the shed on the grounds outside where the other girls were usually housed, chained to the rafters so that they were barely on their tiptoes, awaiting their auctions. They kidnapped three or four girls a week, he told her, usually picking them up in bars or nightclubs. He explained that the first thing they did was strip the girls to make sure they didn't have anything on them that could be tracked. That's why Chloe was in her bodysuit when she woke up.

Even though he was her captor, Chloe had come to think of MD as her protector. He alone could stop Chloe from being auctioned off to sadistic millionaires on the dark web. He alone was trying to secure the funds that would convince Black Death to let her go free.

Every now and then, MD left the house, telling Chloe he was driving to where there was reception so that he could check on the status of her ransom payment. He warned her there would be grave consequences if she tried to escape, and she believed him. Chloe was completely reliant on MD to keep her safe and she obeyed every instruction he gave her. She didn't know if cameras had been set up to watch her, or if other people were keeping an eye on the house. In any event, MD had told her they were too far away from anything for her to run.

MD would invariably come back from these excursions frustrated with the lack of progress on obtaining the money. He told Chloe that if Black Death didn't get the money soon, she would have to be prepared to be auctioned. A doctor would come and check her over for STDs and pregnancy, and more photographs would be taken so that the bidders would know Black Death still had her captive.

By the third day, Chloe noticed that the conversations were beginning to change. Rather than being all about business, MD was beginning to open up and tell her about his earlier life in the military and how he came to be an assassin. He told her he had earned US$15 million from Black Death so far, and Chloe realized he was trying to impress her.

Chloe Ayling was no stranger to men falling in love with her. A large part of her job working as a hostess at events or attending exclusive clubs at the invitation of the owners was to appear approachable and available. She knew she was meant to lead men on and keep them on the hook, so that they would spend more money at whichever establishment they were at. A constant annoyance was men, usually in their thirties or older, interrupting her lunch or workout to talk to her. They often followed her down the street until she invented a boyfriend to get them to back off.

It came quite naturally to Chloe to pick up on MD's apparent growing affection for her and respond in a way that kept him on the hook. She was sweet and agreeable, warm and affectionate. As she murmured sympathetically and responded with feigned admiration at his tales, he talked more and more. He told her that he wanted to get out of the Black Death organization, but that to do so, he would have to pay them $US1.5 million and transfer all of his twenty properties to them.

When they weren't talking, they played Hangman and Battleship to pass the time. MD's demeanor became warmer and less formal and Chloe began to feel less like a business transaction to him. Chloe tried to humanize herself more by talking about her mother and her son, and how much she missed them. The more MD spoke, the more it felt like he believed there was a bond between them, and Chloe knew she could use that to her advantage. If she could make him fall in love with her, she knew he would do anything to stop the auction.

By the Friday morning, four days after her abduction, MD began to talk about a possible relationship, and he asked her if they could share a kiss. Chloe told him that was a possibility once she was free. He started making plans on how they would get Chloe away if they couldn't get the ransom in time. MD believed that if she agreed to promote Black Death in London, where they didn't yet have a strong presence, they might agree to put her on an "untouchables" list.

Chloe promised MD that they would have a relationship after they managed to get away from the clutches of the Black Death group and she was free. She would kiss him, and more, then.

Chloe told the police that this was how she finally convinced her captor to let her free. She had made him believe they would be in a relationship afterwards. MD said she had to arrange €50,000 in bitcoin to be paid, or Black Death would come after her again. She had instructions to advertise Black Death when she returned to London. They knew where her mother lived and they would be watching her every move until the debt was paid.

8

CRACKS IN THE TALE

Plain-clothed officers transported Chloe to the police station. She walked past MD, who was still surrounded by armed guards, and looked into his eyes. She didn't know what was going to happen to him, but she felt sorry for him. He was the only one who had helped her after the Romanians had kidnapped her. He came to her rescue and got rid of the two men who had driven her to the farmhouse. Chloe felt grateful to MD, and she was terrified about what his superiors would do to him if he was arrested.

The rest of Monday was a blur to Chloe. She was questioned about every minute detail of her story and subjected to a thorough medical examination. The police photographed her wrists and ankles and carefully examined the tiny pinhole they found in her wrist. She was made to do a urine test and they cut off a clump of her hair to send for forensic testing.

Everything Chloe told the police was recorded, analyzed, queried, and clarified. It took a long time, because everything also had to be translated. Chloe had arrived at the police station in the morning, and she was still being questioned well into the night. The information she provided was relayed to investigators, who were following up everything she said immediately.

She told them about the letter Black Death had sent her, via MD, to secure her release. The letter said: "You are being released as a huge generosity from Black Death Group. Your release does, however, come with a warning and you should read this letter carefully." She'd had to agree, upon getting home, to "cease any investigation activities related to your kidnapping" and "agree to sneak a predetermined set of information in to the media." The letter went on to say: "You and your family will in no way ever talk about us in bad language and without respect. You have been treated fairly, with respect, and we expect to hear exactly the same about us in return." The letter finished with a demand that she pay "outstanding costs of your release of 50,000 euro", which was to be paid in bitcoin. "Any sort of disobedience with the above will result in your elimination."

Chloe told police that she believed there were five men involved in her kidnapping. There were the two who snatched her, the ones that MD had called low-level Romanian employees. Then there were the two men who had taken her to the farmhouse— the silent masked man, and the man who had gotten into the trunk of the car with her and had a similar accent to MD. Then there was MD himself, the highest level of Black Death out of the five, who had arrived at the farmhouse and taken over from the two men.

At some point, Chloe learned the real name of her captor. It was not Andre Lazio or MD. His name was Lukasz Herba. He was a Polish national who had previously lived in the UK. The name meant nothing to Chloe.

It was around 1:00 a.m., after Chloe had been answering

their interrogations for nearly fifteen hours, that one of the officers hit her with a question she hadn't been expecting. Why hadn't she told them about the shoes?

———

Milan police had been busy while Chloe had been telling her tale. They had followed up all of her claims and worked out where she had been held. The farmhouse was in a tiny hamlet of derelict houses in Borgial, close to the village of Lemie, near Turin. MD, or Lukasz, as he was now known, had lied to Chloe about crossing the border and holding her in Germany. The village was tiny enough that locals had noticed the young Polish man with the modern car who had rented one of the rundown houses for twenty days. He did not own the farmhouse, as he had told Chloe.

The closest town where Lukasz could buy get food and supplies was Viu, a fifteen-minute drive away. Viu was a picturesque little alpine town with a grocery store, cafes, and shops. It was busy during the ski season, but at this time of year it was a sleepy little hamlet. When police showed photographs of Lukasz and Chloe to the shop owners, several of them recognized Lukasz right away. At this time of year, any strangers stood out, and Lukasz had been in to buy groceries and have pizza at the local pizza restaurant nearly every day that week, inevitably taking leftovers with him.

The owner of the mini-mart told police that Lukasz had been in three or four times alone. However, on Sunday morning, he had a girl with him. The owner identified Chloe from the picture police showed her, and said she thought they were a couple, as they wore matching track pants and white T-shirts and held hands. The girl had been standing outside, unguarded, while the man had shopped for fruit, the shopkeeper's son told police.

Police questioned every store owner and discovered another odd occurrence. Lukasz and Chloe had gone to a shoe shop, where Lukasz bought a pair of trainers for Chloe for around €40. That shopkeeper had not noticed anything strange about the couple either.

Italian police gathered CCTV footage from the area. There they were—Chloe Ayling and her alleged kidnapper holding hands and walking closely as they went shopping in the village.

This evidence contradicted Chloe's assertion that she had been held captive the entire time and had not been allowed out of the house. Police were very keen to hear what the young model had to say about her shopping expedition.

When confronted with this inconsistency, Chloe burst into tears. It was difficult to explain, she said, and she had been grilled for so many hours that she didn't want to open up a whole new line of questioning.

When she had convinced her kidnapper to let her go, the plan had been to drop her off a twenty-minute walk from the British Consulate. When she had been abducted, the kidnappers had removed her jacket, jeans and shoes and left them in the abandoned store. Although she was able to borrow a tracksuit from Lukasz, she would not be able to walk that far in his shoes, as she was a tiny size 5.

Lukasz said he would take her shopping for shoes that would allow her to walk the couple of miles to the consulate. On the Sunday morning, she was allowed downstairs and out of the farmhouse for the first time. They went to the local village, with Lukasz reiterating that Black Death operatives were everywhere and could be anyone. She was afraid that if she screamed or tried to get the attention of someone, that person could be a Black Death operative, or they could see her and stop Lukasz from setting her free. What's more, she couldn't speak Italian and she was afraid that she wouldn't be able to make herself understood. Chloe said, "Even if I were free of Lukasz, I would not be free of Black Death."

Chloe said that she firmly believed that Lukasz was her only hope of escape and she wanted to keep him on her side. He had to believe that there was a chance of a relationship once she was freed in order to keep helping her. She held his hand and acted as though she liked him, but in reality she was brainwashed and terrified.

Chloe said that the visit to the shoe shop was brief. She pointed to the first pair of trainers she saw and bought them in a size 6 as they didn't have her size. She never spoke to the shop owner. On the way back to the car, they bought some fruit from the grocery store and then went back to the house for the final night before she was due to be released.

The plan to drop her off twenty minutes away was abandoned when they arrived in Milan two hours before the British Consulate was due to open. Instead, they went and had breakfast and Lukasz told her the new plan, which was to say he was a friend who she had called when she had been released. Apparently he expected to be able to walk rout of the consulate once Chloe had been seen to.

The investigator looked at Chloe coldly as she sobbed. He asked her how she expected him to believe anything she said.

Chloe wasn't allowed to have her cell phone—the one that had been found with her belongings in the fake studio

—and she had to provide investigators with the passcode to unlock it. The police told her that she wouldn't get her phone back as it was being entered into evidence.

The police finally stopped questioning Chloe, but advised her she would not be allowed to leave Italy until the investigations were complete. She would be sent to a safe house, where victims of crime (mostly domestic abuse) were housed. She would stay there until they decided to return her passport.

9

LUKASZ HERBA

While Chloe was being questioned, Lukasz Herba was telling his own story.

At first, Lukasz stuck to the story that he had cooked up over breakfast at the nearby cafe while they were waiting for the consulate to open. He said he was a friend whom Chloe had called when she had been released, and he had come to get her and take her to the consulate. He had tried to leave, but had been detained for questioning, and then arrested for his role in the plot. Police discovered a false ID on him. It was in the name that had been used to rent the abandoned shopfront that he had told Phil Green was his studio. He also carried a business card that bore the business name "Permanent Solution" with a logo of the Grim Reaper on one side, and a complicated dark web email address on the other side.

Lukasz Herba then admitted to being part of the plot to kidnap Chloe, but said his role was limited to renting properties around Europe, including the shopfront and the farmhouse. He said the kidnapping had been orchestrated by a group of Romanians who paid him £500,000. The only reason he agreed to take part in the plot was because he had leukemia and needed the money to pay for medical treatment. When pressed on his illness, Lukasz was unable to provide the names of his doctors or give any other evidence he was sick.

What was missing from Lukasz Herba's story was any mention of the Black Death group.

C hloe's pathology tests came back quickly. Her urine contained no trace of drugs, suggesting that she had not had any within the previous couple of days. However, her hair tested positive for ketamine, a horse tranquilizer that is also used recreationally, meaning that she'd had the drug some time earlier. The puncture mark on her wrist was consistent with the wound that would be made by a needle from a syringe. The bruises around her wrists and ankles were consistent with her having been handcuffed for an extended period.

Italian police held a press conference, naming Chloe and providing details of her story about a kidnapping by the mysterious Black Death group, followed by her miraculous escape. The British press quickly picked up the story and ran it alongside the raunchiest of Chloe's social media photographs. It didn't take long before the public was raising serious doubts about the veracity of the story. The press clamored for an interview with the young model, but she continued to be held by the Italian police. After the first night, they moved her from the safe house to a hotel next to the British Consulate.

Chloe's lawyer told her that the Italian police would not allow her to go home until she had provided them with all the evidence they needed. This included being videotaped taking investigators through the various locations where she had been held.

A couple of days later, a remarkably calm Chloe pulled on blue forensic gloves and took the police on a tour of the locations of her kidnapping.

First she took them to the fake studio and showed them where she had been grabbed, describing exactly where she was attacked. Then she took them to the village where they had gone to buy shoes, retracing the route she and Lukasz had taken, from where he parked the car, to the shoe shop, and back to buy fruit.

It wasn't until she brought detectives to the house where she had been held captive that Chloe broke down. The house was in Borgial, a hamlet of steep hills and ramshackle houses. The house where she was kept was not nearly as remote as Chloe had been led to believe. There were houses either side that appeared to be occupied. They were close enough that, had Chloe screamed, neighbors may have heard her. Composing herself, Chloe took the investigators on a tour. Everything was exactly as she had described it, right down to the colors of the three bedspreads.

D uring the following week, Chloe heard that Lukasz Herba had been badly bashed in prison by other inmates because of his involvement in a crime of violence against a woman. She felt sorry for him when she heard that, and afraid for herself. With Lukasz in prison, who would protect her from Black Death?

The answer came toward the end of the week, as she prepared to give recorded testimony in court so that she would finally be allowed to go home. Police advised Chloe that she did not have to fear Black Death coming after her, because there was no Black Death. In fact, from their investigations, they suspected there were only two people involved in her abduction—Lukasz and his brother Michal Herba. There were no Romanians. There was no second team who took over. Lukasz and Michal had abducted her. Michal was the man who had climbed in the trunk with her and Lukasz was the masked man who never spoke. He was not her savior. He was her abductor.

Chloe was never going to be auctioned on the dark web. Lukasz had kidnapped her in the hope of getting a ransom for her, but he had also become obsessed with her over the past two years. By posing as her savior, he was hoping that Chloe would fall in love with him and the two could start a relationship.

He had told her that he had never been to England, but he in fact lived there. His neighbors knew him as a guy who was obsessed with computer games and walked around with a pet rat on his shoulder. He referred to himself back home as "Vampire Zero God."

The Black Death group was a hoax. In the article in *Motherboard* two years earlier, the journalist had revealed that the photographs he saw on the website were stills taken from a pornographic film. There was no shadowy group running around Europe enslaving women and selling them to be raped and fed to tigers by deranged millionaires. There was just Lukasz Herba and his obsession with one Page 3 model.

Chris Monteiro of the Pirate.London blog tracked down the email address that had appeared on the card Lukasz Herba had produced offering his services as a mercenary, and discovered that that same email address had been used by someone calling himself "MD" looking for work as a hitman in 2016. Back then, he had posted on dark web site overchan.market:

> Hi all,
>
>   New to forum, new to deep web. Find it pretty straight forward.
>
>   I am trying to use deep web capabilities in order to promote very specific service I have to offer.
>
>   6 years military, spetsnaz experience
>
>   5 years private military company experience or mercenary if you wish
>
>   Service: hitman, with full middleman implementation, or as you call it escrow.
>
>   I already know that all hitmen services are scams, I want to promote my own name.
>
>   Where do I start?
>
>   Niche market, I am aware, but I did that in the name of values that were never mine, I shall do it for personal gain instead.

Nobody took him seriously despite his protestations and he was soon trolled off that site. But if he had searched around the dark web around that time, he may have come across the Black Death site. From there, he apparently built up a fantasy world in which he was a highly ranked operative and assassin for the shadowy organization.

It emerged that Lukasz had also emailed the *Daily*

Mirror two days after Chloe had been snatched, with the subject line: British model kidnapped by Russian mafia." He had offered to sell them the story and photos of Chloe. Chloe claimed to have no knowledge of this.

When Chloe testified in court, a curtain hid her from Lukasz so that she didn't have to face her kidnapper. When the court was satisfied, she was finally allowed to fly home. Her former boyfriend Rory met her at the airport and the UK paparazzi was camped outside her house. She and Rory devised a statement for her to read out.

Chloe greeted the press with a smile, playfully scratching her dog's ears, bouncing around the garden and posing for the camera before reading out the prepared statement in a monotone voice. She said, "I've been through a terrifying experience. I feared for my life, second by second, minute by minute, hour by hour. I am incredibly grateful to the Italian and UK authorities for all they have done to secure my safe release." After a few more smiles and poses, she went back inside.

The press crucified her. Chloe did not behave the way they thought a victim should. As far as she was concerned, it was a happy occasion. She had been free for a week, she knew there was no Black Death waiting in the shadows ready to harm her or her loved ones, and she was back home with her mom, her son, and her dog.

Both Chloe and Phil have since written memoirs about the ordeal. In some respects, their recounting of events matches up, but in others, they differ markedly. In *Confessions of a Model Agent,* Phil claimed he had done everything in his power to assist Chloe. In *Kidnapped: The Untold Story of My Abduction*, Chloe said that her mother told her Phil was extremely unhelpful, and even told her to stop calling him when she was trying to find out where her daughter was.

Writing about the time Chloe had to stay in Italy after her abduction, Phil said: "Her lifeline was me and my phone calls to her which she pleaded me to do two or three times each day. Each call lasted up to an hour, and sometimes longer."

Chloe remembered it differently, writing: "We had to call Phil, as he had to book the hotel for me. I had no other way of doing it. I had no choice." She blamed Phil for her predicament. He had not done the checks she thought an agent should have done before sending her overseas to meet an unknown photographer. One telephone call would have confirmed that the studio and photography agency didn't exist.

10

A STRANGE KIND OF CELEBRITY

By the time Chloe had returned to the UK, Phil Green's phone was ringing off the hook with offers for the young model, offering ten times the amount she was used to commanding. He phoned Chloe over and over again, but she never took any of his calls. The one time her phone answered, a man unceremoniously told Phil that he was her new agent and Phil had been fired.

Phil was hurt and angry. He claimed to be out of pocket for expenses related to the kidnapping and believed he had been Chloe's main support during the ordeal. He took his frustration to the interview circuit. "I'm hacked off because Chloe has had the most amazing year with the agency," he told TV presenter Jeremy Kyle.

Every news service ran with the story of Chloe's return home from her abduction, and all of them made sure to include pictures of Chloe taken from her Instagram account —the saucier the better. The public backlash was swift and vicious. The press, and then the public, were quick to note that her demeanor was not what they would have expected from someone who had just been through a traumatic experience. Chloe was clearly lapping up the attention and she did not act the way the public thought a "real" victim should act.

Chloe's new agent was negotiating higher and higher fees for interviews with her. The shopping trip was referenced over and over, each time with accompanying CCTV stills of Chloe and Lukasz walking hand in hand, and other photos taken from Chloe's social media where she was often wearing high heels and little else. Chloe and Lukasz's previous meeting in Paris was reported as "Chloe knew her kidnapper." The press had a field day when they discovered Chloe had accepted Lukasz Herba's Facebook friend request two years earlier.

The press who were unsuccessful in securing interviews were the most vicious. Every headline had the words "kidnap" and "victim" in inverted commas, suggesting they were not accurate descriptors. They couldn't call her an outright liar in case of defamation proceedings, but they made it obvious what they thought.

From earning chump change for her glamour modeling previously, Chloe was suddenly earning big bucks. She did the rounds of all of the high-profile interview shows, including *60 Minutes*, where she outright blamed Phil Green, her former agent, for her kidnapping, because he had not carried out thorough checks of Andre Lazio before sending her overseas. US talk show phenomenon Dr. Phil raised doubts about her story, saying to her, "If this was a publicity stunt gone wrong, the time to say so and stop this runaway train is now." She reiterated that she had been brainwashed into believing Black Death was everywhere and Lukasz Herba was her only hope of escape. She explained their Facebook friendship by saying that she accepted every friend request, because the more friends she had, the higher her profile.

Most interviewers treated her story with cynicism, but stopped short of calling her an outright liar. On *Good Morning Britain*, for which she was paid £5,000 for a twelve-minute interview, Piers Morgan subjected her to a tirade of skepticism bordering on abuse. In this, as in all of her interviews, Chloe came across as unemotional and aloof. When she wasn't posing for the camera with pouted lips, she seemed to have the glimmer of a smirk. Her refusal to become emotional and her blatant willingness to exploit the situation for maximum publicity and income did not sit well with the public. She was labeled an attention seeker whose only validation came from being photographed and talked about.

11

TRIALS AND PUNISHMENT

Lukasz Herba went to trial in February 2018. On the first day, he entered the courtroom smiling and looking relaxed. He was led into a cage, where the accused would usually sit, but his lawyer soon convinced the court to allow him to sit next to her at the defense table.

When the press started printing rumors that Chloe had been involved in her own abduction, Lukasz and Michal Herba's stories promptly changed as well. Lukasz told the court that Chloe had been complicit in the plan from the start, and had helped him write the messages from Black Death to her agent. He said: "She wanted to be a model and she wanted to go on reality TV. She said she wanted to raise her profile, and that it would be useful to her career to create a scandal. She needed help, and so I decided to help her. She had a site where if you paid money you could see spicy photographs. She has no money, so I said I would help her. I hoped that at the end she would remember me, and we could be together. I loved her."

The defense argued that the whole thing was a setup by Chloe, with whom Lukasz had become infatuated. They pointed to the fact that they had been Facebook friends since March 2015, and showed the CCTV footage of the two of them holding hands in the village.

The grocery store owner's son testified that Lukasz had come to the store several times to buy fruit and vegetables, and that Chloe was with him once and had waited outside, unguarded.

A neighbor of the farmhouse where Chloe was held claimed that he had seen her with Lukasz at least twice, and that, from a distance, it looked like they were a couple.

In his testimony, Lukasz claimed that he had told Chloe about the plan when she was in Paris, but she had not liked the place he had proposed to keep her, which was why he changed the location to Milan. He also said he had invented the Black Death group and created a fake website where women were advertised to the highest bidder. He admitted describing himself as a killer-for-hire who had worked for the FBI, CIA and Mossad, and that he had made up the story about the Romanians hiring him to kidnap Chloe for auction.

Lukasz's story changed continually and he didn't seem to notice when he contradicted himself, which was often. He vehemently denied that he had ever told Italian police he had leukemia. In fact, he was so delusional that his lawyer requested a mental health assessment partway through the trial.

Chloe Ayling did not have to testify at Lukasz's trial. Instead, the court relied on testimony she had given shortly after her release, before she had returned to England. Gianluca Simontacchi, the chief investigator, testified in court that Chloe was clearly shaken by the trauma she endured. He did not believe she was complicit in her own kidnapping.

He testified to all the physical and DNA evidence that backed Chloe's story.

The prosecution led evidence gained from Lukasz's electronics that he had planned the kidnap plot months ahead. He had ordered the ski masks and gloves shortly before Chloe's abduction. He had repeatedly googled "Chloe Ayling," "Black Death," "sex-trafficking," and "ketamine" on his personal computer. Lukasz had also phoned his mother from prison, apparently unaware that all phone calls were recorded, and asked her to destroy the evidence—dump his car and delete his emails. He gave her his password to his computer, which was "twattwatI," meaning that investigators had no trouble accessing his files.

They found correspondence and text messages between Lukasz and his bother Michal. One text message said: "Buy a big trip bag. Very big. You know for what purpose it serves so you know how big it should be." In another message, Michał said that Lukasz should be kind to Chloe, because she would be more willing to cooperate.

Lukasz Herba was convicted of kidnapping Chloe Ayling on June 11, 2018 and sentenced to sixteen years and nine months in prison. The court found no evidence that Chloe had been complicit in her own abduction.

This ruling should have meant total vindication for Chloe. The press, however, preferred the narrative that Chloe had masterminded it all. They continued to shed doubt on Chloe's involvement, with headlines like "British Model Chloe Ayling Helped Write Her Own Ransom Note." Only buried a few paragraphs in would the article explain that this was simply one of Lukasz Herba's many claims, and was not backed up by any other evidence.

If Chloe Ayling had truly masterminded her own abduction, she was thorough to the point of genius. The medical examination found bruises from extended periods in handcuffs on her wrists and ankles, a puncture mark from a syringe in her arm, as well as traces of the drug ketamine in her system. The photograph that accompanied the supposed advertisement showed her with her eyes half-closed, pupils dilated. Both her and Michal's hair were found in the trunk of the car. Her DNA was found on the handcuffs, as well as on the floor and the bed where she said she had been held. The Herba brothers could not provide a single record of any messages, emails or telephone calls between her and them, nor were any found on Lukasz's computer.

Chloe's story never wavered and every detail she gave police was checked by the authorities and found to be true and correct. Police, investigators and the court authorities in two countries, who had access to all the evidence, believed her. The British press and public, who had access to her Instagram account, didn't. Many simply refused to believe that someone who looked and acted like Chloe could have been the victim of a violent crime. They wanted to punish her for the image she portrayed, and Chloe defiantly continued to capitalize on her new notoriety.

She competed on *Celebrity Big Brother*, for a fee rumored to be £75,000, where she was the second person voted out and embroiled in a scandal with a married contestant. She also ran into trouble with the lawyer who assisted her in Italy, Francesco Pesce. Chloe claimed in her book that he had insisted on representing her for free. However,

Francesco clearly didn't recall saying that, as he later took her to court for £9000 in unpaid legal fees.

The father of Chloe's son gave interviews saying Chloe had not been to visit her son since she had returned from Italy, preferring to travel the world and cash in on her sudden fame.

In June 2019, in the days leading up to Chloe's testimony by video link in the trial of Michal Herba, Chloe posted increasingly risqué photographs of herself, apparently in a bid to garner more interest in her latest venture. In May 2019, Chloe had started a new job with an adult website, Studio66tv, charging horny punters £2 per minute to watch her strip and engage in "sexy chat." In the teaser clips online, she rolls around on a bed giggling into the phone and touching herself suggestively. In some, she is wearing the same pink bodysuit that she wore throughout her kidnapping ordeal.

In December 2019, Michal Herba was given the same sixteen-year sentence that his brother had received. In January 2020, an Appeal Court reduced Lukasz's sentence by nearly five years, to twelve years and one month. The court found that Lukasz "acted out of love" because he didn't "abandon her in an isolated area" when he released her after six days but drove her to the British Consulate in Milan instead.

Every UK newspaper that reported the story included a line about a threesome Chloe had recently taken part in with two other celebrities.

Chloe's Instagram following continues to grow, with her pictures becoming increasingly raunchy during the coronavirus lockdown. She has also started an Onlyfans account, where punters can pay $15 per month for exclusive, sizzling photos and videos of the glamour model. She continues to be a favorite of the UK gossip magazines.

Chloe was also paid a substantial fee for her book, *Kidnapped: The Untold Story of My Abduction*. In her book, Chloe writes: "Every single word printed in this book is the truth. If you still think this is a fictitious story that I have made up because I'm an attention seeker, I suggest you read something else. I don't have time for your or your skepticism. Going through what I have gone through has taught me one thing: you never know what is going to happen; you never know what is round the corner. You have to live every moment."

APPENDICES

1. Transcript of the 9-1-1 call made by Stephen Allwine

2. Transcripts of the emails from Stephen Allwine to "Rita's Playhouse"

3. Unedited transcripts of all emails between "dogdaygod" and Besa Mafia

4. Website of the Black Death group

TRANSCRIPT OF 9-1-1 CALL

Below is an unedited transcript of the 9-1-1 call made by Stephen Allwine to report his wife's apparent suicide.

Start date: Sunday, November 13, 2016, 19:00:22

"DISPATCHER": Washington County Sheriff's Office
"ALLWINE": Stephen Carl Allwine, victim's husband
"CHILD": Victim's son

DISPATCHER: 9–1-1, what's the address of the emergency?
ALLWINE: I think...
DISPATCHER: Hello.
ALLWINE: ...I think my, I think my wife shot herself. There's blood all over.
CHILD: Shot herself, with a gun?
ALLWINE: (Speaking to son): It looks like it.
DISPATCHER: Okay, what is your address, sir?

ALLWINE: Hang on. It's 7624. (Speaking to son): All right, come here.

DISPATCHER: Does she still have the gun, sir? Sir?

ALLWINE: Yes.

DISPATCHER: Does she still have the weapon?

ALLWINE: I don't know. We just got home.

DISPATCHER: Where did she shoot herself?

ALLWINE: I don't know. I just saw her and, and blood.

DISPATCHER: Okay. Do you see her right now?

ALLWINE: No, I'm with my son in (unintelligible) house.

DISPATCHER: Okay. Where is she located?

ALLWINE: She's in the bedroom. (Speaking to son): Come here, bud.

DISPATCHER: Okay. Sir, do you know if she was breathing at all?

ALLWINE: I don't.

DISPATCHER: Okay.

ALLWINE: We just got back from dinner.

DISPATCHER: Okay, would you like to check on her and see if she is, or do you believe that she's beyond help?

ALLWINE: (Speaking to son): Stay, stay there for just a second.

CHILD: Why?

ALLWINE: They want me to go check on her. Hang on.

DISPATCHER: Just don't touch any of the weapons or anything like that, but I just need to know if she's breathing and where she shot herself, okay?

ALLWINE: There's blood. The weapon's by her.

DISPATCHER: There's no weapons by her?

ALLWINE: There is, there's the gun. And...

DISPATCHER: Where? Okay.

ALLWINE: ...she is not breathing. I, I can't tell where she's shot. I don't know.

DISPATCHER: How long ago do you think she shot herself?

ALLWINE: I was here, um, um, when did I leave? Uh, I did...

DISPATCHER: Sir, if you'd like to exit the room to make it easier for you, you can do that, okay?

ALLWINE: ...uh, 5:00, about 5:15, 5:30, I.

DISPATCHER: Okay, so you last seen her around 5:00, 5:30?

ALLWINE: Yes.

DISPATCHER: How old is your, how old is she?

ALLWINE: 43. (Speaking to son): Come here.

CHILD: Is she? Oh, why did she do this?

ALLWINE: (Speaking to son): I don't know. I don't know, bud. Come here.

DISPATCHER: I know that this is really hard, okay?

ALLWINE: (Speaking to son): Here, grab the green (unintelligible) or somethin'. (Unintelligible), come here. I don't know, bud.

CHILD: Are you gonna remarry?

ALLWINE: (Speaking to son): (Laughs) I don't know, bud.

CHILD: I'm just sad.

DISPATCHER: Are there any other weapons in the residence, sir?

ALLWINE: Yes, there is a, a shotgun in the room and, uh, two rifles downstairs.

DISPATCHER: Okay. Is the shotgun the one she has?

ALLWINE: No, she had a handgun.

DISPATCHER: Okay.

CHILD: Why you calling the police?

ALLWINE: (Speaking to son): It's 9–1-1.

CHILD: (Unintelligible) police shoot (unintelligible).

DISPATCHER: I'm gonna stay on the line with you until my officers arrive, okay? You're doin' a really good job. What is your call back number?

ALLWINE: 6-, (Speaking to son): No, they don't need it, bud. 651–253–8105.

DISPATCHER: What is your first name?

ALLWINE: Steve.

DISPATCHER: Is it Stephen by given?

ALLWINE: Yes.

DISPATCHER: Okay, and your last name?

ALLWINE: Allwine, A-L-L-W-, A-L-L-W-I-N-E. (Speaking to son): There you go, bud.

CHILD: (Unintelligible). (Crying)

ALLWINE: (Speaking to son): I know.

DISPATCHER: Where are you located in the residence?

ALLWINE: We're, we're in my son's room on the other side. It's o-, over by the garage.

CHILD: I am just so sad. (Crying)

DISPATCHER: Is it just you and your son home right now?

ALLWINE: Yes.

DISPATCHER: Okay.

CHILD: Oh, mommy, (unintelligible) see what is happening to me.

DISPATCHER: You're doing a really good job, Stephen, okay?

ALLWINE: (Crying)

CHILD: (Unintelligible).

DISPATCHER: Stephen, are you able to just step out of the, step out of the home with your son so my Officers can see when they pull up?

ALLWINE: Yeah. (Speaking to son): Joe, can you get a hoodie or something, we must get out of the house.

CHILD: Why? (Unintelligible).

ALLWINE: (Speaking to son): Just put one of mine on for now, bud.

CHILD: (Unintelligible)?

ALLWINE: (Speaking to son): The police are gonna come in and take a look.

DISPATCHER: And, Stephen, I'm gonna stay on the line with ya until they arrive, okay? Let me know when they, when you see them.

ALLWINE: (Speaking to son): Come here.

CHILD: (Unintelligible).

ALLWINE: (Speaking to son): I don't either, bud. (Unintelligible). I see a tru-, it looks like a truck, I can't tell.

DISPATCHER: That's okay; they'll approach you, okay?

CHILD: It's disgusting.

ALLWINE: (Speaking to son): I know.

CHILD: I'm sad. I (unintelligible) good memories. Well, I feel bad. Can I go in and get the earmuffs?

ALLWINE: (Speaking to son): Yeah. (Coughs).

DISPATCHER: Are you in the front of the garage there, Stephen, or where are you?

ALLWINE: My son wants to get (unintelligible) he doesn't like loud noises. He's worried about that.

CHILD: (Unintelligible).

ALLWINE: (Speaking to son): You don't have to, though. (Unintelligible). Hello?

DISPATCHER: Hello.

ALLWINE: Uh, it looks like they just arrived. (Speaking to Officers): She's over in the bedroom, on the far side.

DISPATCHER: Okay, I'll disconnect with you, Stephen, okay?

ALLWINE: (Speaking to Officers): I couldn't tell.

DISPATCHER: Bye-bye.

ALLWINE: (Speaking to Officers): I, I didn't look.

End date: Sunday, November 13, 2016, 19:08:08

EMAILS TO RITA'S PLAYHOUSE

Following are the emails between Stephen Allwine and "Rita" of Rita's Playhouse police found on his computer. Long before he decided to kill his wife, this "Man of God" was cheating on her with at least one sex worker. His browsing and email history suggested that he visited or contacted several different online dating or sex work services.

Stephen used the email address grin55077@yahoo.com.

Sent: Thursday, July 24, 2014 7:48 PM
From: grin55077@yahoo.com
How much for an overnight for Friday Aug 1?

Sent: Thursday, July 24, 2014 8:02 PM
From: ritasplayhouse@yahoo.com

Hello,

I can tell you that history was my favorite subject in school. And my favorite American statesman was Benjamin Franklin, who is honored on our $100 bill. A writer, an inventor, a founding father and a diplomat. Would you be agreeable to including all 4 of those topics in our overnight of private conversation?

Pleased to meet you, I'm RITA :-)

Sent: Thursday, July 24, 2014 8:44 PM
From: grin55077@yahoo.com

I am sure you are excellent tutor, I look forward to our lessons. I assume we can do the lessons at your place, since you probably have all the appropriate materials there. Let me know if that does not work.
Steve

Sent: Thursday, July 24, 2014 8:52 PM
From: ritasplayhouse@yahoo.com

Yes, Steve. I like to meet friends at my private, quiet and cozy residence in CR. What timeframe were you thinking for our lengthy conversation? 7 pm through 6 am? RITA

Sent: Thursday, July 24, 2014 9:05 PM
From: grin55077@yahoo.com

That should be fine. I will be driving in from the Twin Cities, so depending on when I get out of here we might have to be a little flexible, if that is OK. Is there a place that you would like to grab a bite to eat. I can take you out, since we cannot study an empty stomach. If we go out, then we could just meet there, get to know each other a bit, and I can follow you back when we are done.

Let me know. Thanks, Steve

Sent: Friday, July 25, 2014 7:54 AM
From: ritasplayhouse@yahoo.com

Sounds good Steve. There's either the sports bar near where I live with pizza, burgers, nibblies, or you can choose Italian, Thai, Korean, Sushi, pretty much anything that you would like.
RITA

Sent: Friday, July 25, 2014 9:01 AM
From: grin55077@yahoo.com

How about Italian? Give me the name of that place and we can meet at 7, if anything changes with my schedule then I will l let you know. I am 6'2", 180lbs, and will be driving a silver Dodge RAM.

Steve

———————

Sent: Friday, July 25, 2014 7:21 PM
From: ritasplayhouse@yahoo.com

Hello Steve,

There's a new Italian restaurant, opened early this year, I haven't been to as yet, but I have heard positive remarks. If you wouldn't mind embarking on the adventure with me, it's Popoli Ristorante, 101 3rd Ave SW, (319) 363–1248, popolicr.com to see menu. It's also very near to where I live, downtown.

RITA

———————

Sent: Monday, July 28, 2014 7:28 PM
From: ritasplayhouse@yahoo.com

Well done on the reservation, Steve. I can taste the tomato sauce and Cabernet Sauvignon already :-)

Also, since you are visiting, I will throw out to you that there are a couple of pool halls near the restaurant (and my place). I don't know if you play or would even be interested, but, in case you were still wound from your drive and wanted to stay out a bit, it's an option. I'm not much of a worthy opponent, but, what I lack in skill I brazenly try to make up for in diversionary tactics <wink>

- Just trying to entertain my guest :-) RITA

Sent: Tuesday, July 29, 2014 8:45 AM
From: grin55077@yahoo.com

Sure, sounds good. Steve

Sent: July 31, 2014 00:59 am
From: grin55077@yahoo.com

Here is my cell number in case we need to connect on Friday, as I will not have access to email while traveling. 347-[REDACTED]

Thanks, Steve

Sent: Tuesday, October 14, 2014 10:22 PM
From: grin55077@yahoo.com

I sent you a text as well, but wanted to check to see if you would be around 11/7. I had a wonderful time with you last time I was in town. I wondered if I could stay over again. You can pick out a nice place to eat or we can stay in and work something up :-)

This time I will stick around all night, as long as you let me get a little sleep. Let me know.

Thanks, Steve

Sent: Wed, Oct 15, 2014 10:52:49 AM
From: ritasplayhouse@yahoo.com

Hi there Steve,

I'd love to have you again ;-) As for the room situation, that's up to you. I completely understand how unsettling it is not having your own bed, bathroom, peace and quiet when you're trying to sleep and get up and get ready to go in the morning.

I look forward to seeing you. Have a good day. Rita

Sent: Wednesday, October 15, 2014 9:07 PM
From: grin55077@yahoo.com

Sounds great. I look forward to it. I will ping you when I am on my way down and maybe meet you at your place after work. I will need your apartment number again, but we can worry about that later.

Have a wonderful day. Steve

Sent: Monday, November 3, 2014 10:58 AM
From: grin55077@yahoo.com

Good morning, I am just checking to make sure that we are still on for Friday. Let me know and assuming we are, then I will ping you when I am on my way down, probably around noon or so.

Looking forward to it, Steve

Sent: Monday, November 3, 2014 3:52 PM
From: grin55077@yahoo.com

Had a thought as to what to do Friday night. If you want to put together some salad stuff, I will get the fixings for lasagna, we can make it up there, stay in and enjoy the food and friendship. :-)

Sound good? Steve

Sent: Monday, November 3, 2014 8:02 PM
From: ritasplayhouse@yahoo.com

Sounds good to me! :-) I'm looking forward to dining upon it... and on you ;-)

Have a good night. Rita

Sent: Monday, November 3, 2014 8:16 PM
From: ritasplayhouse@yahoo.com

What time do you think you'll be in town, by the way?

Sent: Monday, November 3, 2014 8:51 PM
From: grin55077@yahoo.com

I will shoot for whenever you're done with work. The food
takes about 30 minutes to prepare and about an hour to
cook, so if you are done at 5ish and I get there then (and if
we do not get too distracted right away), then we would be
eating about 6:30 or so. So you let me know when you
usually get home and I will plan accordingly.
The sooner the better in my mind ;-) Steve

Sent: Wednesday, November 5, 2014 8:12 AM
From: ritasplayhouse@yahoo.com

Good morning Steve,

Yes, 5 pm sounds good :-)

Can you give me a heads-up as to recipe so I can have things
on hand? I already have a full bulb of garlic. Plus I have
most spices. I don't have Oregano though, in case that's in it.
What all should I have here? That way we're not
duplicating.

I have a nice, big, stoneware lasagne cooking dish + Pam
spray. And I have a bottle of Merlot and a bottle of Asti

Spumante if either might appeal to you? Or I can pick up
some beer or any other thing to have cooling in the fridge.
Rita

Sent: Monday, November 5, 2014 14:46 PM
From: grin55077@yahoo.com

I usually use the following ingredients:
pound of ground beef
package of lasagna noodles
jar of spaghetti sauce (I usually get the roasted garlic)
mozzarella cheese
cheddar cheese sour cream Italian seasoning Onion
maybe some mushrooms if we want to go crazy :-)

Let me know what you do not have and I can bring it down.
The merlot sounds great.
I am excited ... this will be fun.

See you in a couple days.
Steve

UNEDITED MESSAGES BETWEEN
DOGDAYGOD AND BESA MAFIA

The following pages are the messages between dogdaygod (Stephen Allwine) and Besa Mafia. This represents the entirety of their correspondence, and **errors in spelling and grammar have been retained from the original**. This can sometimes make for frustrating reading, but I thought it was important to reproduce these messages faithfully.

Sent: 2016–02–15 03:28:55
From: dogdaygod@hmamail.com
To: besa@sigaint.org
Subject: Bitcoin Anonymously

I am looking to hire you for a hit, but what is the recommended way to convert cash to bitcoin anonymously. If I pull $5000 out for a hit, after the hit I would assume that the police would see that draw and wonder where it went, so even if the bitcoins are not traceable, that missing money would raise suspicion? Is there a way to make it look like I am buying something and end up with bitcoins, so that the money looks like it is going to something tangible and not cash to pay for a hit?

Sent: 2016–02–15 11:55:11
From: besa@sigaint.org
To: dogdaygod@hmamail.com
Subject: Re: Bitcoin Anonymously

Hello,

You can exchage money to Bitcoin on coinbase.com and localbitcoins.com

We will plan a date together for the hit when you can travel outside of the city for a day or two, this makes everyone know what you coukd not be the murderer

Regarding Bitcoin, yes you can say you have purchased a gaming server that costs $5000 online, with games such as Metin or similar game, and we can provide you with access to one of our money laundering gaming servers, for a limited period.

You can tell everyone that you invested in online games for children, and they could not proof you din't and you are safe.

Let me know

Sent: 2016–02–16 06:43:38
From: dogdaygod@hmamail.com
To: besa@sigaint.org
Subject: Target location and BTC cost

The target will be traveling out of town to Moline, IL in March, but that is about 3 hour drive from Chicago. I am assuming that this would not work for the hit? If it would then it would be the perfect time. Also, you give the price in USD$, but then say that we pay in BTC. What is the price in BTC for hit and ideally making it look like an accident?

Sent: 2016–02–16 16:46:49
From: besa@sigaint.org
To: dogdaygod@hmamail.com
Subject: Re: Target location and BTC cost

Hi. Yes, this will work fine for the hit. You will need to tell us exactly the address in Moline, Il where the target will go, for the hitman to know where to wait him, and a date when he will be at that address. Our assigned hitman will watch the address and kill him on sight.

Regarding the price, normal killing by gun shot is $5000 . That is 13 Bitcoin. Killing by gunshot is the easiest and cheapest, This is basic killing by a gang member who will use a turtle neck and a handgun, he will shoot the target from close range. Targets are usually shot when they go to the car, or get out of car, in parking lots, etc

Killing to make it look like accident, is $5000 + max $4000 , depending on what kind of accident you want to simulate.

Our gang members in the Il can wait him at the location and run him over by a stolen car, or run into his car to the driver side, making it look like an accident. This costs $6000.

We usually need a picture, a place where he will be and date .

Then you add Bitcoins to your Private Walled on your acount.

Upon seeing the funds available, we will assign a gang member from the town to do the job. We will give all information to him and he will do it as per your specifications.

The bitcoin will stay into your account until the job is done, and then you send it to the assigned hitman.

Sent: 2016–02–16 19:48:00
From: dogdaygod@hmamail.com
To: besa@sigaint.org
Subject: Re: Re: Target location and BTC cost

Hit and run is what I was thinking would be the easiest "accident', and that would work fine. So can we say 15 bitcoin for hit with a car and ensure fatality?

I am in the process of exchanging and tumbling coins.

Thanks

Sent: 2016–02–16 21:12:55
From: besa@sigaint.org
To: dogdaygod@hmamail.com
Subject: Re: Re: Re: Target location and BTC cost

Yes, 15 Bitcoins for hit with a car and ensure fatality.

If you need help or advice in getting bitcoins let me know

Sent: 2016–02–18 13:46:32
From: besa@sigaint.org
To: dogdaygod@hmamail.com
Subject: Bitcoin exchanging

Hi,

Please be carefull when tumbling coins, use trusted mixers.

Is not very mandatory to tumble bitcoins as we have our internal coin mixer to break traces and bitcoins are scrambled

How is going? If you need any assistance please do not hesitate to ask

Sent: 2016–02–29 17:33:07
From: besa@sigaint.org
To: dogdaygod@hmamail.com
Subject: how is going?

Hello, Just a quick follow up: how is going? Can you aquire the bitcoins fine? Let me know

Sent: 2016–03–05 03:42:49
From: dogdaygod@hmamail.com
To: besa@sigaint.org
Subject: Re: how is going?

Yes, I have the bitcoins now. I would prefer to use a third party escrow service. Is there one that you have dealt with in the past?

Sent: 2016–03–05 04:25:40
From: dogdaygod@hmamail.com
To: besa@sigaint.org
Subject: Escrow Service

It looks like Bitrated will work. I need to give them a username or email on bitrated.com I also need to give them a product or service and method of delivery. An recommended thoughts on wording? I would suggest product is training or consulting or purchase car, but not sure what a good description would for arbitration. I assume you have worked through this before, so you probably have better ideas. Thanks

---

Sent: 2016–03–05 12:51:14
From: besa@sigaint.org
To: dogdaygod@hmamail.com
Subject: Re: Re: how is going?

Hello,

In the past we have used our Bitcoin Escrow service. Please note Besa Mafia is an website where gang members and killers can join, and where customer give orders. Besa Mafia is acting like an intermediary between the customers and the gang members and hitmen.

Besa Mafia is receiving 20% of the payments done to hitmen; ex. for $5000 the gang member actually gets $4000 and $1000 goes to us

We protect our customers, and our gang members from those who want to do fraud.

Regarding escrows, we can not reccommend any external escrows, because you could accuse us of being "on-the-hand" with the reccommended escrow; you could acuse that we own that escrow or control it.

If you want to choose an external escrow; then you are trully free to do so and we accept, but it needs to be your reccomendation of an external excrow, not ours

Take care

Sent: 2016–03–05 12:56:31
From: besa@sigaint.org
To: dogdaygod@hmamail.com
Subject: Re: Escrow Service

Bitrated is a reputable escrow service. However I do not know if they allow murder for hire, you can contact them from an anonymous email and ask them.

Regarding a product or service as method of delivery, we must specify murder for hire; and the target details. If our gang members claim they did the job, escrow should be able to verify that the person is dead; either from the news (when they are shot dead they usually get into the news) or from a local check.

We can not say consulting or purchase of a car, because after our gang members kill the person, you could claim that you got no car, the Bitrated staff sees you got no car, and they would return the bitcoin to you; you could get the murder for free.

And as you are anonymous, we could not do anything to you.

Please find a reputable escrow that allows illegal things, like drug trade, prostitution, organs traffic, murder for hire, unregistered guns, and then tell what escrow you want to use

Take care

Sent: 2016–03–05 16:27:57
From: dogdaygod@hmamail.com
To: besa@sigaint.org
Subject: Re: Re: Re: how is going?

Can you explain to me how your escrow service works, because all I see when I go to deposit money is a bit coin address, which could be a personal address? I want to trust you guys, but I do not understand how I have any control over the money once I send it to you to ensure that the project is done. I assume you can understand my concern. When I go to "my account" with you, where does that address go, do I have to give approval that the job was done for it to leave that account, etc

Thanks

Sent: 2016–03–05 16:57:09
From: besa@sigaint.org
To: dogdaygod@hmamail.com

Subject: Re: Re: Re: Re: how is going?

Hello,

Yes, ofcourse. Each customer has his own Bitcoin Wallet on our site. Each gang member and hitmen has his own account with his own Bitcoin wallet on our site.

This Besa Mafia site is operated, hosted and administrated by the cyber team of Besa Mafia; we get 20% of the payment that goes to hitmen and gang members.

When you deposit money you send it to your Bitcoin Address. It takes several minutes or more to reach up a defined number of confirmations, and our automated system then puts the Bitcoin into your account.

You can see it at the top right side of the screen.

When you have the entire amount of money added up to your Account on Besa Mafia, we wil assign a hitman as per your specifications.

Hitmen get a notification that you have the Bitcoin into your account on Besa Mafia.

They do the job as per your requirement, and when done, they will provide us with proof; usually depending on the murder; local news reports will pop up on the Internet about the murder.

Once you verify that the hit has been done, you give us OK to send the payment from your account to the hitmen account.

We will retain 20% of the amount, and the hitmen gets %80 of the amount. This is how the Besa Mafia deep web site division makes money; and we have albanian members, russian members, and other gang members who have active accounts on our site.

If the assigned hitmen fails to do the job for any reason;

we can either assign an other hitmen to your job; or you can move the funds out from your account;

As you trust coinbase.com and other online sites with your Bitcoin, you can trust BesaMafia .

You need to either trust us, or you need to trust some external Bitcoin escrow that accept illegal things, and provide it to us; however please notice that they must be reputable or the same question will arise there - how to prevent them from stealing your funds.

I hope you can trust us, and I can assure you that is in our best interest to have happy customers; we will make a lot of money in the long term if customers are happy and recommend our services

Let me know if this is ok with you

Sent: 2016–03–05 18:11:02
From: besa@sigaint.org
To: dogdaygod@hmamail.com
Subject: bitcoin rate

Hello,

As you might have noticed, the bitcoin exchange rate sometimes goes up, and other times it goes down, as any other exchange rate

Our official policy is to use the Bitcoin exchange rate the day when it was received to your account on Besa Mafia; my advice is, if you are fine with using our escrow wallet, would be good to send your existing Bitcoins to your private wallet on Besa Mafia before drops down more; as this cause to consider the existing echange rate of today.

If bitcoin rate goes futher down, you won't lose any more

money; or else you will have to buy additional bitcoin. This is just a thought and reccomendation, you can do as you feel best :)

If you decide to use an external escrow; do your research on them before the rate goes futher down; usually bitcoin have fluctuated in past months between $360 to $430 or more.. up and down.. a 30$ down in bitcoin rate, at 12 bitcoins is about $400 , a $60-$70 drop in bitcoin, at 12 bitcoins is about $1000.

Bitcoin is used by many people as an investment; they do money by knowing when to sell and when to buy, hence the variation in price

I do hope you will trust us, and understand it's in our own interest to have thousands of happy customers and make large amounts of money.

While we don't get thousands of killing orders, we do get thousands of revenge orders for beating up; set fire to cars, damaging cars or properties; as people usually revenge on each other, and is not good if unhappy customers give us bad reviews or reputation

Let us know Take care

Sent: 2016–03–06 01:49:18
From: besa@sigaint.org
To: dogdaygod@hmamail.com
Subject: bitcoin personal address

Hello,

As an addition to my previsious messages, yes the bitcoin address you see is your personal bitcoin address on your Wallet.

Your wallet has several bitcoin addresses, where you can multiple payments. All the funds you send will build up to show your account balance.

Please sinup on coinbase.com and localbitcoins.com , on each site you have your own bitcoin personal address.

Let me know

Sent: 2016–03–06 01:55:55
From: dogdaygod@hmamail.com
To: besa@sigaint.org
Subject: Trust

OK, I did some research and everything that I read says that you are real and can carryout what you say you can do. They say that Besa means trust, so please do not break that. For reason that are too personal and would give away my identity I need this bitch dead, so please help me.

Thanks

Sent: 2016–03–06 02:34:05
From: besa@sigaint.org
To: dogdaygod@hmamail.com
Subject: Re: Trust

Hi,

Yes, Besa means trust and we don't dissapoint our customers.

I see you have added 15.5 Bitcoin to your account.

Please place your order by clicking on the Order button,

and give us the specifications, I will see a good available hitmen in the state of your target that can do the job with no problems.

Please also tell us a date when you want the hit to be done, it is best for you to travel away from the city if you live in the same city with the target.

Our hitmen won't leave any evidence at the scene of the murder, and is better for you to be out of town on that day, preferably in a different city where you can be video recorded by some public cameras in like a library or some Mall at shopping.

This is to avoid any possible suspicious that you went there to do the murder yourself; is good to be able to say that you were traveling to a different city to buy some clothes or relax on that date, and the distance should be far enouch that they know you could not be able to drive back into your city to do the murder.

You need to clean up your computer with some Privacy Software; and with this you are 100% protected, no one can suspect you are involved let alone prove anything.

Let me know

Sent: 2016–03–06 03:06:40
From: besa@sigaint.org
To: dogdaygod@hmamail.com
Subject: Order

Ok, We got the order details.

The assigned hitman will schedule to do this job in the night between 19th to 20 march.

He will wait her at the airport, tail her with the stolen

car, and when he has the chance will cause a car accident to kill her.

He will have his gun with him, if by any chance the car accident goes wrong and she doesn't die, he will shoot her deadly.

He will try his best to make it a car accident and make sure she dies in the impact

Do you know, is there anyone else scheduled to come with her at the airport? Like companion, anyone?

The hitman want to knows if she is scheduled to be alone or if he should be careful about companion, is not a problem if she has companion but is good to know, to be prepared.

If she has companion, they might both die in car accident, you need to be sure is not someone with her that you might feel sorry for, like a offspring or some relative that you care about

Let us know

Sent: 2016–03–06 15:10:52
From: dogdaygod@hmamail.com
To: besa@sigaint.org
Subject: Re: Order

She will actually be driving down from Minneapolis through Cedar Rapids to Moline. She will have a companion with her, but no one that I care about.

Sent: 2016–03–06 15:31:58

From: besa@sigaint.org
To: dogdaygod@hmamail.com
Subject: Re: Re: Order

Hi,

Ok, Got it and noted down.

The informatin has been given to the assigned hitman; he will expect them at the location on the date.

We will keep you posted

Take care

Sent: 2016–03–14 19:09:54
From: besa@sigaint.org
To: dogdaygod@hmamail.com
Subject: remember good alibi

Hello,

On march 19 please make sure you are sorrounded by people most of the days, and spend some money to shop things on malls or public places where they have video surveilance.

This way you ensure that no one can ask you where have you been on march 19

Our killer won't get known, so the identity of the killer will be unknown, police will do some checks to see if any ennemies could have been at the scene of the accident to cause the accident

If you have good alibi, they can't do anything else than say it was accident and close it

Let me know

Sent: 2016–03–16 15:16:19
From: dogdaygod@hmamail.com
To: besa@sigaint.org
Subject: Re: remember good alibi

Thank you for the reminder. I will make sure I have a good alibi.

Sent: 2016–03–16 18:43:45
From: besa@sigaint.org
To: dogdaygod@hmamail.com
Subject: Re: Re: remember good alibi

Hi
    Ok

Sent: 2016–03–20 21:35:05
From: dogdaygod@hmamail.com
To: besa@sigaint.org
Subject: Re: Re: Re: remember good alibi

I have not seen anything, do you know if this is done?

Sent: 2016–03–20 21:59:57
From: besa@sigaint.org

To: dogdaygod@hmamail.com
Subject: Re: Re: Re: Re: remember good alibi

Hi,

No not yet. The hitman has followed her, but he did not had the chance to do the hit yet, he needs to be in a position where he can hit her car to the driver door, lateral collisin to make sure she dies. Other types of impact myght have her remain alive, which is not good.

In worst case scenario this can be done by a sniper, shot her to the head and that's it.

If that would be the case; would anyone suspect you of anything? Because if not, a sniper hit would be greatly recc-ommended

Let me know

Sent: 2016–03–20 22:34:22
From: dogdaygod@hmamail.com
To: besa@sigaint.org
Subject: Re: Re: Re: Re: Re: remember good alibi

No, I would not be a suspect. I am fine with whatever you think is best.

Sent: 2016–03–20 23:30:10
From: besa@sigaint.org
To: dogdaygod@hmamail.com
Subject: ok, options to do this

Hi,

Ok. I got comunication with the hitman on spot, and he told me that he can do the accident hit; however if she does not die he will need to run away; depending on the situation it might be difficult to check if she died or shoot her if she din't, and risk being not able to leave the spot because of damaged car after shooting She doesn't drive too fast, and she din't put herself in vulnerable spots, the hitman saith in this conditions success rate is about %60 if he forces the hit

Option 2, using sniper. Usually a sniper hitmen charge $30 000 for a hit, and they have 100% success rate. However because you are already a customer, and we want to do this with 100% success rate, I got a hitmen who can drive to her in 2 hours, to do the hit for $12,000 , that would be rounded down 10 bitcoins difference.

Let me know if you are interested to upgrade to the sniper hitmen option for 10 bitcoin with 100% success rate, or if you would like to proceed with the curent order for existing 15.5 Bitcoin paid, accident murder; 60% success rate because of the short time spawn (only a few days) and place

Either way, is fine with us; a third option, if you want to cancel the hit, we can send you the bitcoin back, as our customer satisfaction is the most important thing for us

Let me know

Sent: 2016–03–21 00:33:45
From: dogdaygod@hmamail.com
To: besa@sigaint.org
Subject: Re: ok, options to do this

I do not have 10 bitcoins handy. I would think that she would need to stop for food or gas at some point can he shoot her then and get away? If not, then we can cancel. I think she makes another trip in a couple weeks to Atlanta, and you could try again there.

Sent: 2016–03–21 00:44:37
From: besa@sigaint.org
To: dogdaygod@hmamail.com
Subject: Re: Re: ok, options to do this

Yes, if she stops for food in some place with no surveilance cameras, the hitman will shoot her.

Ok, if he doesn't have a good change of doing the accident, or shooting her without being caught on camera; until she leaves, then we will give you a refund.

Alternatively if you have $4000 available, you can exchange it to bitcoin on localbitcoins using 4–5 traders simultaneusly, and you can get it done within in several hours

If you do not have the cash or would not want to pay for the sniper, that is fine; the hitmen will do his best to hit her and be able to flee from scene uncaught, or a full refund.

Let me know

Sent: 2016–03–21 00:47:29
From: dogdaygod@hmamail.com
To: besa@sigaint.org
Subject: Re: Re: Re: ok, options to do this

I do not have the cash available at the moment, so yes. If she stops and he can get her there then do that. If not, then I will take a refund and place a new order when I find out her new travel arrangements.

Sent: 2016–03–21 04:07:50
From: besa@sigaint.org
To: dogdaygod@hmamail.com
Subject: Re: Re: Re: Re: ok, options to do this

Ok.

We don't usually ask this, because we are not interested in the reason for why the people are killed, but if she is your wife or some family member, we can do it in your city as well; making it look like accident or rubbery.

Doesn't have to be away from home, you can leave the city too, when we plan to kill her at home

Let me know

Sent: 2016–03–21 18:43:33
From: dogdaygod@hmamail.com
To: besa@sigaint.org
Subject: Re: Re: Re: Re: Re: ok, options to do this

Not my wife, but I was thinking the same thing. How much would it be to kill her at home, and then burn the house so that they cannot tell if anything was stolen or not (I am not sure if they have anything worth stealing)? I am not certain that she will be going on the future trip. This Thursday I know she will be home between about 9 and noon Central time. Her home address is 7624 110th St S, Cottage Grove, MN, 55016 (near Minneapolis)

Sent: 2016–03–21 21:50:59
From: besa@sigaint.org
To: dogdaygod@hmamail.com
Subject: Re: Re: Re: Re: Re: Re: ok, options to do this

To kill her at home, and burn the house afterwards would be 10 extra Bitcoins, and the success rate is 100%.

Let me know

Sent: 2016–03–22 00:21:28
From: dogdaygod@hmamail.com
To: besa@sigaint.org
Subject: Re: Re: Re: Re: Re: Re: Re: ok, options to do this

OK, I can get that together. I will have it on the site tomorrow, if not tonight.

Sent: 2016–03–22 01:27:36
From: besa@sigaint.org
To: dogdaygod@hmamail.com
Subject: re: options

Hi,

Ok.

Let me know

Sent: 2016–03–22 14:53:27

From: dogdaygod@hmamail.com

To: besa@sigaint.org

Subject: HELP! wrong bitcoin address

My screen refreshed and gave me the wrong bitcoin address where I sent the other funds. Are you able to match them up? It went to 1FUz1iECnhN2Kw8MUXhZWombb-w1TCFVihb

---

Sent: 2016–03–22 14:55:33

From: dogdaygod@hmamail.com

To: besa@sigaint.org

Subject: Maybe it is OK

I do not see the funds yet, but it looks like that bitcoin address changes each time, so maybe it is OK

Sent: 2016–03–22 21:33:05

From: dogdaygod@hmamail.com

To: besa@sigaint.org

Subject: Schedule

OK, I got some more details on her schedule. I am trying to get as much as I can without being obvious. It looks like she will be home tomorrow from 12- 1PM and Thursday from 12–1PM. Those are the only times that know about at the moment. Let me know the plan so I can be somewhere else public. I know her husband has a big tractor, so I suspect that he has gas cans in the garage, but I do not know that for sure. She usually drives the Sienna so if that is there she should be.

Sent: 2016–03–22 21:43:53
From: besa@sigaint.org
To: dogdaygod@hmamail.com
Subject: Re: Maybe it is OK

Hello,

Yes, all new bitcoin addresses are yours.

I have checked and the bitcoin has credited to your account.

Sent: 2016–03–22 21:47:25
From: besa@sigaint.org
To: dogdaygod@hmamail.com
Subject: Re: Schedule

Hi,

Good, this information is very helpful. We schedule the hit on thursday at 2 PM .

He hitman will go there, do the job, and if there are also

gas canisters in the garage that is very helpful. Our guy will bring some gas canisters with himself; in case the canisters in the garrage are empty or missing; he will put his canisters there and the police will think that the canisters were already there for the tractor; as everything will be badly burned and won't be able to get any traces from the burned canisters

---

Sent: 2016–03–22 21:53:16
From: dogdaygod@hmamail.com
To: besa@sigaint.org
Subject: Re: Re: Schedule

Can he do it closer to 12? I am not sure if she will be around at 2PM? I heard that she will be there from 12–1 working on her computer, because she is watching some event.

Sent: 2016–03–22 23:40:19
From: besa@sigaint.org
To: dogdaygod@hmamail.com
Subject: Re: Re: Re: Schedule

Ok, I have rescheduled it to be done at 12. The hitman has been updated
    If you find out any changes in her planes, Let me know

Sent: 2016–03–23 04:41:39

From: dogdaygod@hmamail.com
To: besa@sigaint.org
Subject: Re: Re: Re: Re: Schedule

OK, Thank You

Sent: 2016–03–24 19:36:32
From: dogdaygod@hmamail.com
To: besa@sigaint.org
Subject: Status

I do not see any status. Do you have an update? I suspect the kid and dad will be home about 4 and then we will need to hold off.

Sent: 2016–03–25 01:07:30
From: dogdaygod@hmamail.com
To: besa@sigaint.org
Subject: What happened?

I gave you guys a good time and good information about her. I talked to her today and she said that she was home at 12. Now her kid is on spring break. I am not sure that we will get a good chance until her kid goes back to school. Are you still able to do this? If so, then I will try to feel her out for another opportunity.

Sent: 2016–03–25 03:49:54
From: besa@sigaint.org
To: dogdaygod@hmamail.com
Subject: Re: What happened?

Hello,

I got update from the assigned hitman. I apologize he could not do the hit today, he had some problems with getting to the location.

Yes, we are able to do this. If you can provide us with a good time and date again, I am sure we will do it properly and won't let you down.

Our customer satisfaction is very important for us; and we can give you a refund if you are not happy, but I do hope that you will provide us with a new date and hour, and the assigned hitman will do it.

Sometimes things don't go as we want them or expect, but with perseverence we will do it; we just want to get it right; she dead + good fire to destroy all evidence and the hitman on job not getting caught

Let me know

Sent: 2016–03–25 13:06:58
From: dogdaygod@hmamail.com
To: besa@sigaint.org
Subject: Re: Re: What happened?

Yes, I do want it done, but I have to pretend to be her friend to get this information and it driving me crazy to be nice to her. I am also afraid that if I dig for information to many more times that it will look strange. I will get another day and time, how much lead time do you need?

Sent: 2016–03–25 19:22:17
From: dogdaygod@hmamail.com
To: besa@sigaint.org
Subject: Monday

It looks like Monday might work. It sounds like the dad is taking the kid somewhere. If so, early morning would probably be most likely for her to be home alone (8:30–10 or so). I will try to get more specifics on times, but let's plan that tentatively.

Sent: 2016–03–26 01:38:32
From: besa@sigaint.org
To: dogdaygod@hmamail.com
Subject: Re: Monday

Ok, monday morning is set.

Our guy will be there at around 8:30 . He already has the extra gas canisters in his truck if there are not enouch canisters in the garrage; and he has everything ready.

If you get information that she changes her plans, let us know. If not, our assigned hitman will be there. This must work.

Let me know

Sent: 2016–03–26 22:52:39
From: besa@sigaint.org
To: dogdaygod@hmamail.com
Subject: Re: Re: Re: Monday

Ok

Sent: 2016–03–26 03:37:36
From: dogdaygod@hmamail.com
To: besa@sigaint.org
Subject: Re: Re: Monday

Sounds good. If the silver truck is not outside, then she
should be alone.

Sent: 2016–03–28 15:59:25
From: dogdaygod@hmamail.com
To: besa@sigaint.org
Subject: missed again

It looks like it did not happen again.

Sent: 2016–03–28 17:54:29
From: besa@sigaint.org
To: dogdaygod@hmamail.com
Subject: Re: missed again

Hello,

Yes, this did not happened this morning because the assigned hitman was stoped by police for a driver and registration check and the car was stolen, he was token in for declarations.

He called his lawyer and declared he purchased the car from the someone without knowing it was stolen, but he still need to give more declarations; he won't go to jail.

However, this might mean that we wil pospone the job for about 3–4 days or more, until he is out

Or, I can assign a different hitman on the job; and would be recommended that he buys a cheap car; so that he does not steals a car for the job, especially as he might need to stay parked in the area. This guy also has an unregistered sniper rifle; and we can make for him fake id; he can buy a car so if police stops him the car will be alright, no stolen car They don't use their real cars because if someone sees the license plates while they drive away, they could give it to police and they could just go pick up the hitman

If they steal just the plates and get stopped by police, they see the plates are not for the car and he stil could be in trouble.

However to do the job by the other hitman, with purchased car for the job, he would need an a difference of 8 Bitcoins , 4 to buy a used car and 4 for the help as he will have an other guy with him; to ensure this gets done

We have two options, either do the job fast by the new assigned hitman with 8 bitcoin extra, or waiting for the previsious hitman get released from custody to go do the job in a week or two

Let me know which one you prefer

————

Sent: 2016–03–28 18:34:49
From: dogdaygod@hmamail.com
To: besa@sigaint.org
Subject: Re: Re: missed again

We can wait. Let me know when he can try again.

Sent: 2016–03–28 19:30:59
From: besa@sigaint.org
To: dogdaygod@hmamail.com
Subject: Re: Re: Re: missed again

Hi,

Ok. in a week or two. we will keep you updated

Sent: 2016–03–31 03:51:27
From: dogdaygod@hmamail.com
To: besa@sigaint.org
Subject: Target

Hello I was very disappointed that the hit did not happen
Thursday and Monday as it was expected to. I realize that
things happen, but this bitch has torn my family apart by
sleeping with my husband (who then left me), and is
stealing clients from my business. I have had to continue to
act like her friend to get information and I cannot do it any
more. I have gone out of my way to try and get you good
information. I feel that I am at risk of being suspected if I

ask too many more questions. You have had three good attempts at her and none of them have worked.

I liked the idea of shooting and fire, because I think it would look like a robbery and cover up, but I am at the point that I do not care how it is done. I believe that if I go about my regular routine that I will not be a suspect, if I stop asking questions and just act normal.

So, I would like to suggest that you have until May 1st to do it in whatever way works best for you and your people. Based on our previous conversations, if it is a straight shoot and kill then it is 13, if it looks like an accident then it is 15, and if it a robbery and fire then it is 25. If it is not done in someway by May 1st then I would like my money back. Does that sound like enough time for you? I cannot get my hopes built up again like I did this weekend by having a date in mind and then have those hopes torn down when it does not happen. So I do not care about date or method, you have her picure and address, so you can tail her or do whatever you need to do to get the job done. I ask that you only get her and not the dad or kid as the kid is a friend of our child's and I do not want to leave him orphaned.

I do know that she is going to take the trip to Atlanta the weekend of April 7 to 10, but I do not know the details. I also was passing by recently when they had the garage door open and I was able to see that they did have 3 (what looked like 5 gallon) gas cans just outside the door from the house to the garage, and what looked like a propane tank as well. I am not sure if any of them are full, but they are there. Thanks for your help with this, I need her out of my life, so I can move on.

Sent: 2016–03–31 07:32:03
From: besa@sigaint.org
To: dogdaygod@hmamail.com
Subject: Re: Target

Hello,

I am really sorry to hear what she did. Yes she is really a bitch and she deserve to die.

Things sometimes happen that is not the way we planned, but with perserverense our assigned hitman will do the job.

May 1st is a good deadline; the asigned hitmen will surely be able to kill her by then.

It's best for you to avoid digging more info about her directly, so that you won't be a suspect, we have enouch information at this point and our guys will find the perfect oportunity to do the job during a month time.

It will be the hitman and a driver gang member, they will be careful not to accidentally harm the kids or other persons when doing this; only the bitch will be killed.

We will keep you updated and we can assure you that we can do this job during the April.

Take care

Sent: 2016–03–31 21:05:47
From: dogdaygod@hmamail.com
To: besa@sigaint.org
Subject: Re: Target

Hi,

I know the feeling when things do not work out as we want it to.

Yes, if it is normal shooting is 13 Bitcoin, if is like accident 15 Bitcoin, if is shooting and setting fire to make it look like robery 25 Bitcoin.

Please notice 80% of our hitman are gang members who do drug dealing, beatings, ocasional murder; few of them have military training and not all have good experience.

I will make sure we put pressure on the assigned hitman to do the job by the 1st May, or a full refund will be given.

If you could afford to spen an difference of 10 Bitcoin, for 35 Bitcoin we can assign the job to a ex-military from Chechenia. He has moved into the USA 4 years ago, and he does ocasional murders for us, he use explosives and he is an expert in hand to hand combat.

He is not hesitant like other gang members; he can kill with cold blood with guns or with bare hands; he doesn't think twice as other people do.

However his price is 35 Bitcoins, and he can kill the bitch within two days from the moment when the funds are in your account; he can make sure no one else is hurt as he follows specifications with extreme care.

I don't know if you can afford to pay the extra Bitcoins to upgrade to this killer, but if you do, we would higly recommend him.

If you don't then is ok, we will put pressure on the existing assigned hitman to do the job by 1st may, or a full refund.

Let me know

Sent: 2016–03–31 21:20:26

From: dogdaygod@hmamail.com
To: besa@sigaint.org
Subject: Re: Re: Target

We should stay with the current hitman and plan.

Sent: 2016–03–31 21:27:25
From: besa@sigaint.org
To: dogdaygod@hmamail.com
Subject: Re: Re: Re: Target

Ok.

Sent: 2016–04–04 03:49:21
From: dogdaygod@hmamail.com
To: besa@sigaint.org
Subject: Re: Re: Re: Re: Target

I happened upon some useful information. Her husband is going on a trip, so she will be alone when her son is at school. April 12,13, and 14 between the hours of 9AM and 4PM. I suspect she will be in and out during those times, but you should be able to tail her on one of those days and be sure that she will be alone when she gets home.

Maybe this helps

Sent: 2016–04–04 08:26:17

From: besa@sigaint.org
To: dogdaygod@hmamail.com
Subject: job and fire

Hello,

Thank you, this is very useful information.

So 13, 13 or 14 is the date when she will die.

I will update the assigned hitman.

Please consider that the assigned hitman only killed once before and it was drug related; he is not with a lot of experience, basically all our $5000 to $10 000 killers are not having a long experience with this.

I still higly recommend for you to do some sort of sacrifice and get the difference of Bitcoin to upgrade to the sniper; if you do that, she will die on 12th for sure, and the house will be on fire.

Let me know

Sent: 2016–04–11 04:41:20
From: dogdaygod@hmamail.com
To: besa@sigaint.org
Subject: Target schedule

Just a reminder that the target should be alone Tuesday through Thursday this week. I also saw that they are giving away their piano, so your person could probably call the number in the ad 6512538105 and setup a time that she will be there. He can say he is calling about the baldwin upright and wants to setup a time to look at it, and that will ensure that she is there.

Sent: 2016–04–11 12:49:20
From: besa@sigaint.org
To: dogdaygod@hmamail.com
Subject: Re: Target schedule

Yes, thank you.

The hitman will be ready for it on Tuesday; and thank for the tip, he will buy a new prepaid sim card to call to ask to see the piano; and make sure the target is there

Sent: 2016–04–13 00:41:32
From: dogdaygod@hmamail.com
To: besa@sigaint.org
Subject: Re: Re: Target schedule

Looks like it did not happen today. I really need this to happen in the next 2 days, it will be the best opportunity for you.

Sent: 2016–04–14 01:58:43
From: dogdaygod@hmamail.com
To: besa@sigaint.org
Subject: Do you have the right guy for the job

Once again, it does not look like it happened today. He has had 2 perfect days to do this and has not gotten it done. Tomorrow will be another full day that he can get this done, and Friday I am sure he would have most of the day as well. Since he has not gotten this done, I have a low confidence level that he will get this done in the next day and a half. I have put my trust in you for the last month and a half and this has not happened. Here is a chance for you to put your trust in me. If the person dies, I am pretty sure that her husband will give or sell me her business in which case I can get some more money to give you. The next day and a half should be perfect with her being alone, so if this happens in the next day and a half, then I will find a way to get you another 25 bit coin after the fact. You have no reason to trust me other than I give you my word of honor, as I have trusted yours.

Sent: 2016–04–14 02:20:01
From: besa@sigaint.org
To: dogdaygod@hmamail.com
Subject: Re: Do you have the right guy for the job

Yes, we do have the right guy for the job.

We have all kind of gang members, from young teenagers who sell drugs and beat people, to ex trained military that wants to do extra revenue by killing.

The prices ranges, depending on their skills.

We apreciate the offer of the 25 Bitcoin after the job; however if you could get us 10 now, and 15 after, I am sure I could assign a different team on the job that would get the job completed tomorrow

The more money is in it, the more experienced the guys who go there.

They look into the Bitcoin on the table, that is the

amount in your wallet; when accepting or rejecting the job, and right now the team there is formed by two drug dealers who are one 19 years old and the other is 24 years old.

They did beating and some jail time; but they do not have the balls to do something without hesitation.

I can call them off and send someone more determined, if there are 10 more bitcoin into your wallet; someone who have been fighting in afganistan and did many killings before

I am not trying to get you pay more money, I am just explaining the situation; I am one of the admins working in the cyber team; there are various gang members on the field and they take jobs depending on the bounty

---

Sent: 2016–04–14 02:42:28
From: dogdaygod@hmamail.com
To: besa@sigaint.org
Subject: Re: Re: Do you have the right guy for the job

I am a single mom, who pulled money out of my business to get this done, because I am pretty sure that I will get her business after it is done, but it would be difficult for me to get more money out of the business at the moment. When it is done, then I will either get her business or the customers that she stole from me will come back and I will have much more money to pay you. Until, it is done the money is very tight. What do you think is the chance they will get this done? It should be easy, she is alone, they are in the country, so no one should see them. If they do it during the day then any neighbors should be at work. I have given you the information to do this the easiest way possible. if they wait, then it will become difficult, because then they will have to start tailing her and looking for a quiet opportunity again. Her husband normally works from home, so once he gets back, then they have to wait for him to go out and for her to be there, there are many more things to work around. If they are going to do it, then they really need to get it done tomorrow, or I think they will end up with nothing, because it will only get harder.

Sent: 2016–04–14 03:03:23
From: dogdaygod@hmamail.com
To: besa@sigaint.org
Subject: more bitcoins

I am sending in about 4 more bitcoins that I had left over, if 10 will get someone that will get it done, then I think you guys owe me the extra 6 for the time that it has taken to get this done, then when it is done i will pay you the 15 extra.

Sent: 2016–04–14 03:06:19
From: besa@sigaint.org
To: dogdaygod@hmamail.com
Subject: Re: more bitcoins

Hi,
    Ok, that sounds fair.

Sent: 2016–04–14 04:46:00
From: dogdaygod@hmamail.com
To: besa@sigaint.org
Subject: bit coins

OK, they should be uploaded now

Sent: 2016–04–14 12:47:52
From: besa@sigaint.org
To: dogdaygod@hmamail.com
Subject: Re: bit coins

Hello,

Yes, we people that make fake ids, including bank statements, driving licenses, ids, etc.

I have also contacted the loan sharks in Ireland and ask them to call you, this has been long and they need to call

Do you think instead to get a fake set of documents and get a loan from a bank?

That might be a good ideea as you won't pay the interest neither the loan bank

Let me know

Sent: 2016–04–14 20:12:42
From: dogdaygod@hmamail.com
To: besa@sigaint.org
Subject: Re: Re: more bitcoins

I uploaded those bit coins, but I do not see them showing in my wallet. Also, my expectation was that if I put those coins up there, that we would get someone else to take care of her today, and yet it does not look like it happened. Is this going to happen today or tomorrow? I sent this last night, but it you replied back with something about fake ids.

Sent: 2016–04–14 21:10:22
From: besa@sigaint.org
To: dogdaygod@hmamail.com
Subject: Re: Re: Re: more bitcoins

Hi,

I am looking now in the bitcoin mixer for any delayed transactions, your bitcoins should show up shortly

I am checking with the hitman, yes this should be done today or latest tomorrow

Let me know

Sent: 2016–04–14 23:25:34
From: dogdaygod@hmamail.com
To: besa@sigaint.org
Subject: Re: Re: Re: Re: more bitcoins

They were sent to 1AAgpuH6PQgPYrGj5HCdPjWh-AM22V1Zvdt 3.929 BTC were sent from one address and .475 BTC were sent from another address between 9:30PM and 10:00PM Central Time

Sent: 2016–04–15 11:43:41
From: dogdaygod@hmamail.com
To: besa@sigaint.org
Subject: Losing confidence

I was told that adding the extra bit coins would get me
someone that could get the job done for sure yesterday or
today and it is now today. I am not sure when the husband
gets home, but I think your guy probably has less than 7 or 8
hours, and I do not see you responding to my messages and
I do not see my extra bit coins in my wallet. Are you going to
be able to carry through on your promise?

Sent: 2016–04–15 12:41:57
From: besa@sigaint.org
To: dogdaygod@hmamail.com
Subject: Re: Losing confidence

Hi I checked the incoming transfers and they are in the
bitcoin mixer, it took longer than usuall to be mixed because
of the wallet from where they came; it will be shown in your
balance shortly
    I checked with the hitman team and they saith they will
do this today

Sent: 2016–04–15 17:13:19
From: dogdaygod@hmamail.com

To: besa@sigaint.org
Subject: Re: Re: Losing confidence

I still do not see the funds and it is now 12:00 and nothing has happened so far. They have about 3 more hours before the window closes.

Sent: 2016–04–16 01:42:25
From: dogdaygod@hmamail.com
To: besa@sigaint.org
Subject: They failed again

What is their excuse this time? Whoever you have is making you look bad. You claim to have honor and you promise and promise and promise and nothing is getting done. They had at least 3 perfect days when she was alone and could not get it done. How am I supposed to believe that it will ever get done?

By the way, I still do not see my bit coins in my wallet

Sent: 2016–04–16 14:13:34
From: besa@sigaint.org
To: dogdaygod@hmamail.com
Subject: Re: They failed again

Hello,

I have checked the bitcoin mixer and the coins should be in your wallet shortly.

I have asked the assigned hitmen for a full report,

including a good explanation for why they failed to do this on the scheduled date. I will get back to you shortly.

If they continue to fail, we will provide you with a full refund, but I hope they wont

Let me know

Sent: 2016–04–16 17:03:15
From: besa@sigaint.org
To: dogdaygod@hmamail.com
Subject: Re: They failed again

Hello,

The bitcoins should be visible in your wallet soon.

Regarding the hitman, I have requested a full report of why they din't completed the job yet

This might go to suspend them; if they continue to fail this you will get a full refund, however I hope they will do it ok

Let me know

Sent: 2016–04–17 00:04:33
From: besa@sigaint.org
To: dogdaygod@hmamail.com
Subject: Re: They failed again

Hi,

Have you received the extra coins in your wallet? Please let me know

Sent: 2016–04–17 01:15:52
From: dogdaygod@hmamail.com
To: besa@sigaint.org
Subject: Re: Re: They failed again

I do see the extra bitcoins now.

You told me in a previous email that if I could get you 10 more (bringing the total in my wallet to about 35btc) then you could assign a different team that would get the job done tomorrow (which would have been 4/14)

I did not have that, but I asked if 4 now and 15 later would work and you said that it sounded fair, which means I expected that a different team would be assigned, and a team that could have gotten the job done on 4/14. As it turns out, they had 4/14 and most of 4/15 and they still could not get the job done.

Regarding the refund, I just want the job done successfully. What good do the coins do, if she ruins my business

After all the time that this has taken, I think you guys owe me someone that we can both count on to get the job done once and for all. Your reputation is on the line, because from what I have seen you do not have the contacts to get this done.

Once you have someone good picked out that can actually get the job done, just tell me when you plan to do it, and I will make sure I have an alibi.

I am tired of waiting and I want this done.

Sent: 2016–04–17 13:26:01

From: besa@sigaint.org
To: dogdaygod@hmamail.com
Subject: Re: Re: Re: They failed again

Hello,

Yes. After you added the 4 Bitcoin I immediately spoke to one of our best teams; is formed by one ex-military member who has experience in war combat, and now retreated; he is working with a guy that is an expert in car stealing and drug dealing.

My hope was to convince them to do the job, I knew if they do it the job would be taken care within same day.

However they refused to do the job saying they don't trust anyone to pay remaining bitcoins after the order is completed; because customers are completely anonymous; and if they would not pay, nothing could get them to pay since no one knows who they are.

I tried to insist but they refused.

I have assigned a different team; more skilled than the first; but less skilled than the above team that I hope to assign.

I know that is fair to assign the best team because of the delay; but unfortunately the gang members and ex-military that do services for us are all for the money; they don't have much ethic code they kill for money

If you can add the difference of 5.6 Bitcoin; as you sent 4.4 and about 10 was the difference to get this excellent team assigned, i can get them assigned and they would do the job within a day guaranteed

If not, I hope the other team that is good will still do it

Let me know

Sent: 2016–04–17 14:33:0
From: besa@sigaint.org
To: dogdaygod@hmamail.com
Subject: Re: Re: Re: They failed again

Hello,

Some of our members saw your comment on reddit; and you din't used public wifi or protection, please notice that is the worst ideea to comment on exteriour sites about you trying to do bad things without having protection. Police is monitoring those threads and can track you down

Also, if you are unsatisfied about our services we can give you a refund.

Please delete your comment, or your comment would result immediate termination of services

Let me know

Sent: 2016–04–18 03:36:45
From: dogdaygod@hmamail.com
To: besa@sigaint.org
Subject: Re: Re: Re: Re: They failed again

I will remove it, but I need you to be successful.

Sent: 2016–04–18 04:06:13
From: dogdaygod@hmamail.com
To: besa@sigaint.org
Subject: Re: Re: Re: Re: They failed again

Comment is deleted, but I NEED you to be successful. As mentioned I cannot pull that out of my business at the moment. I guess I will hope your other team is successful. Please give me a heads up when they are planning to do it, so I can have a good alibi.

Sent: 2016–04–18 04:07:53
From: besa@sigaint.org
To: dogdaygod@hmamail.com
Subject: Re: Re: Re: Re: Re: They failed again

Hi,

Yes, we will be succesful, but you can remove that before we do it.

Polices look over threads like that and try to locate users who say "i've tried them" and might track you, so regardless if we are succesful or not, it's still best for you to remove it.

People won't be scared off by that comment, they could think it's an undercover cop doing it anyway so it doesn't help much

let me know

Sent: 2016–04–18 04:07:57
From: dogdaygod@hmamail.com
To: besa@sigaint.org
Subject: Wallet

My wallet is back down to 25.5, the 4.4 that I added is gone. That makes me nervous that money is disappearing from my wallet without my approval.

Sent: 2016–04–18 04:11:43
From: besa@sigaint.org
To: dogdaygod@hmamail.com
Subject: Re: Wallet

Hello,

The last transaction got again mixed in our internal bitcoin mixer, as our programmers fixed some issues with the bitcoin mixer and this caused all last transactions to be remixed.

So the bitcoin went back into the mixer, got remixed, and should be back into your wallet shortly

let me know

Sent: 2016–04–18 04:13:06
From: besa@sigaint.org
To: dogdaygod@hmamail.com
Subject: Re: Re: Re: Re: Re: They failed again

Hello,

Thank you

I have asked the team to give me a time estimation, and to make a good plan this time to succeed without any trouble or delays.

I will let you know shortly of what they say

Yura

Sent: 2016–04–19 18:40:09
From: dogdaygod@hmamail.com
To: besa@sigaint.org
Subject: Re: Re: Re: Re: Re: Re: They failed again

Any news from them?

Sent: 2016–04–19 23:01:52
From: besa@sigaint.org
To: dogdaygod@hmamail.com
Subject: Re: Re: Re: Re: Re: Re: Re: They failed again

Hello,

Thank you for deleting the comment.

They did not completed the job yet, but I asked them to complete it in max 24 hours

if they don't complete it we will give you a full refund, but we hope they will complete it

Let me know

Sent: 2016–04–20 03:02:38
From: dogdaygod@hmamail.com
To: besa@sigaint.org
Subject: Re: Re: Re: Re: Re: Re: Re: Re: They failed again

Please get it done. You have promised this before, so I guess I
will believe it when I see it (or hear about it)

Sent: 2016–04–20 22:02:58
From: dogdaygod@hmamail.com
To: besa@sigaint.org
Subject: How will you get this done

Orginally on Feb 16 (over 2 months ago) you said that it
would be 13 btc to have a close range shot (shot going to or
coming from her car) Then you said that hit and run would
be 15 btc. "Yes, 15 Bitcoins for hit with a car and ensure fatality." You then ensured me that this would happen on Mar
19th You indicated that she was being followed, but he did
not have an opportunity with the car. The accident was a
secondary objective not the primary objective. It is hard to
believe that in that weekend there was not some opportunity to do the close range shot. You then recommended a
sniper and I said that was fine. You said it would be an additional 10 btc "Let me know if you are interested to upgrade
to the sniper hitmen option for 10 bitcoin with 100% success
rate" At the time I did not have it, but I have since added that
and more. You followed that with the option of the home
"To kill her at home, and burn the house afterwards would
be 10 extra Bitcoins, and the success rate is 100%." Indicating
that both of these are 100% success rate. We have a 0%
success rate now with 2 different teams, and being at this for
a month.

Mar 22nd was a fail Mar 26th was a fail - you said our
guy will be ready at 8:30 You had from then until April 12 to
follow her and do a close shot You indicated "So 13, 13 or 14 is

the date when she will die." (I think you meant the 12 April 12 was a fail April 13 was a fail April 14 was a fail You said "however if you could get us 10 now, and 15 after, I am sure I could assign a different team on the job that would get the job completed tomorrow" You were sure you could get someone that could do it on the 15th. I did not have 10, but I had 4+ and you were going to cover the rest to get us to that mark of 10 to get someone that you were SURE could do it on the 15th

"Hi,

Ok, that sounds fair.

I am sending in about 4 more bitcoins that I had left over, if 10 will get someone that will get it done, then I think you guys owe me the extra 6 for the time that it has taken to get this done, then when it is done i will pay you the 15 extra."

You said "yes this should be done today or latest tomorrow"

April 15 was a fail

You said "f you can add the difference of 5.6 Bitcoin; as you sent 4.4 and about 10 was the difference to get this excellent team assigned, i can get them assigned and they would do the job within a day guaranteed" Based on our previous agreement you were going to front the 5.6 btc to get the "excellent" team, but apparently that did not happen.

Again on the 18th you claimed "Yes, we will be succesful"

You said that you asked your team " to make a good plan this time to succeed without any trouble or delays." and "I asked them to complete it in max 24 hours"

Yet here we are at the end of another day with another broken promise.

Please remember that the house, the accident, etc is all secondary goals. The primary goal is her and has always been her. I think people are getting so tied up in the secondary goals that they are forgetting the primary goal.

I do not care how it is done, but based on our discussions over the last 2 months, I believe that I have added enough for - close shot - hit and run with car - snipper - burn house - better team - excellent team (with you filling in the other 5.6 as we discussed)

And yet it is still not done. What are you going to do to get the job done and get it done right?

Sent: 2016–04–21 01:17:50
From: besa@sigaint.org
To: dogdaygod@hmamail.com
Subject: Re: How will you get this done

Hello,

First I need to apologize. You are right, this has been dragging quite a long time, and needs to be completed asap.

I will explain a bit why this has been so haotic, even if maybe you don't want to hear excuses, you want to hear that the jobs has been completed, and see her dead.

When our website was first launched in 2013, we had only albanian members on board; and our network was only made of old good albanian people living in USA and Europe; doing mostly drug dealings and ocasional beating up, murder etc; for drug related debt or other purposes. Taking orders on the website was a way to extend the revenue, and it was great.

The initial prices for shoot and run was between $10 000 to $20 000, and we had ex military people who did sniper hits on lawyers, business man with bodyguards, etc for prices between $50 000 to $120 000 .

The team managing the site was receiving %20 of the hits, just as it is receiving now. So the gang members doing the hits are geting %80 and the team of people runing the server, doing programming, admins here, etc are getting %20

This is our internal stuff

Then we had the ideea to accept new gang members, many new gang members, anyone who did our test order to beat someone or do some bad thing was accepted. Many teens in 17–19 years old were accepted.

Our old gang membeers were taking the high paying jobs, while the low paying jobs were given to the new members, who many times din't had the skills or experience to do the hits well.

This is why we lowered the price to $5000 for basic shoot and run.

Many of these new inexperienced gang members did the shot and run job well. If you google for shoot dead news you wil find hundreds of news about people being shot in the streed by unknown persons who come, shoot and run, no argument no fight no nothing, all these are paid people who shoot; they have no reason on their own they are just paid

However, many don't have the guts to pull the trigger when they are in the place, it's not so easy to kill someone if you don't have experience

So, long story short, the failure so far was because the teams so far did not have a lot of experience, and because maybe your target was lucky

When you put a price on the job; we have an internal system that shows your job and price to a selection of hit teams; and they can apply to get it; then we assign it.

If we assignt he job to a very expert hitman, he can just refuse it, and we can't force him to do the job

This is why I adviced you to increase the bount repedly. I know that for what you added so far, you are entitled to a good hit and as soon as possible

But if the existing teams at this price can't do it soon enouch, then I can only recommend you to make a little effort if you can, to get some loan from someplate, add some more bitcoin and this will become appealing to some expert hitman who will go there and kill her ass off in one day

Either this, or we can offer you a refund; we don't want to have a complaining customer that scares away 100 customers, is better to refund 1 customer and get 500 new customers by end of year, than to have 1 complaining customer and lose 500 new customers by end of year or more

So, please do the best you can to add some extra bitcoin and an expert team wil be attracted and go there kill her in one day.

Sent: 2016–04–21 02:05:28
From: dogdaygod@hmamail.com
To: besa@sigaint.org
Subject: Re: Re: How will you get this done

BTC to USD is about 1 to 437, which means I have over \$13000 in there at the moment. That is in that \$10-\$20K range. I want to be a happy customer. This should be an easy job, when her husband leaves, she is at home alone at the end of a dead-end street, there is no one around to hear. This is not a job in town where there are lots of neighbors.

She has huge property. This is an easy job, which is why I do not understand why it takes so long. At the end of the street people always park and sit down there to smoke or watch the scenery, so it would not look strange to have someone wait down there. so you have your guy sit down there until the end of one of her classes and when she goes back to the house you take care of it. I was talking to her this evening and she volunteered her schedule for tomorrow (thankfully she still thinks I am her friend). She has a class from 9:00–10:30, there is something at her son's school at 11:30 (so she would be home from 10:30–11:30 … your guy could watch for all the cars to leave and then follow her back to the house), she has to be back for a class at 1:30 (which means that she should be home about 12 or so, he could sit at the end of the road and watch for her green van to pull in the driveway and do it), then she should be home about 3 or so in the afternoon (once again, sit at the end of the road and watch for her van).

She said her husband is out running errands tomorrow. I know you do not know me and have no reason to trust me, but I do not know you and have no reason to trust you and yet I have trusted you with $13000. Reading online it sounds like many hits pay half up front and half after, so if you want a happy customer, and it cost more to get a good hit, then you add that to my account (as a loan), and I will pay up to 15 more when it is done. If the husband gives me the business then I could get that 15 to you immediately, but if he does not I will still pay back it just might take longer. I believe in honor that is why I have trusted you. She has dealt with me very dishonorably which is why I have got to this extreme. I want her gone, I NEED her gone. Please help me

Sent: 2016–04–22 01:10:08
From: besa@sigaint.org
To: dogdaygod@hmamail.com
Subject: Re: Re: Re: How will you get this done

Hi,

Yes, you are right.

However the more skilled team won't take the job until they see you have the extra 6 Bitcoins available, you sent 4 from 10 so if you could send other 6 they would take it

I know we should do this with the existing amount, so I will put more pressure on the existing team to do it.

Other than that, there is nothing else that I can do, except that if they fail I can provide a full refund

I told the more skilled team that you will send 15 bitcoins after the job is done; but they don't think much and they only go for what they see ready

Let me know

Sent: 2016–04–22 04:59:34
From: dogdaygod@hmamail.com
To: besa@sigaint.org
Subject: Re: Re: Re: Re: How will you get this done

Can your team provide some evidence that they are actautly surveilling and doing something to prepare, either photos or descriptions that they would only know if they were surveilling her? I am not convinced that they have done anything. I feel like I need to stay involved to get you information, but I would like to keep my distance so I am less of a suspect, but if I cannot trust that they are doing their job, then I feel like i have to do it for them. Can you at least get proof from them that they have done something and know something about the target? It sounds like she will be alone most of the afternoon tomorrow (Friday), because her husband and child are planting hundreds of trees in the back field. They would not be able to hear a shot from way back there.

Sent: 2016–04–22 05:04:12
From: dogdaygod@hmamail.com
To: besa@sigaint.org
Subject: Re: Re: Re: Re: How will you get this done

My understanding of our discussion about the 10 extra bitcoins, was that I would add 4 to my wallet and you would add 6 to my wallet so that 10 showed up and then they would do it. I added my 4, but you never added the 6.

Sent: 2016–04–22 19:44:30
From: besa@sigaint.org
To: dogdaygod@hmamail.com
Subject: Re: Re: Re: Re: Re: How will you get this done

Hello,

Yes, I agreed to your proposal and I have forwarded it to my superior; he rejected it.

Please notice that our site has several admins (6 in total) to be able to answer and provide support 24/7, and one supervisor (the 7th person) who is above us all.

We, the admins and the supervisor do not do any jobs our selfs and we all answer to a bigger boss.

The teams doing jobs are all registeted on the site and we comunicate with each other through this secure encrypted enviroment.

I agreed to your proposition and I took it to my superior, or boss if you want.

He rejected the proposal of adding the additional 6 Bitcoin into your account from us; because if you don't pay, the team doing the job will get the money and we lose it.

The boss saith that if the team fails to do the job, you get all your money back. Either the current amount or the bigger amount, if you add the extra 6 Bitcoin.

He suggested that I put more pressure on the assigned team, and if they continue to fail they will be suspended and not take future orders through this site; also you get a full refund .

We have two options, either you manage to add a difference of 6 bitcoin and assign the superior skills team that gets this done in 1 day, or option 2, we put more pressure on the existing team and hope they will do it.

Let me know

Sent: 2016–04–22 21:58:43
From: dogdaygod@hmamail.com
To: besa@sigaint.org
Subject: Re: Re: Re: Re: Re: Re: How will you get this done

For now put more pressure on the team that is supposed to be doing it. As mentioned I would like some evidence that they are doing something. If they are watching her, then they should be able to provide picure evidence or a description that indicates that she is being watched and they are ready when there is an opportunity.

Since the husband was planting trees this weekend. I suspect that she should be home alone again on Monday when he takes the planter back. It usually takes him all day.

Sent: 2016–04–23 00:22:48
From: besa@sigaint.org
To: dogdaygod@hmamail.com
Subject: Re: Re: Re: Re: Re: Re: Re: How will you get this done

Hi,

I have sent them a message requesting them that they send a picture or description of what is going on there.

As soon as they provide I will send it to you

Let me know

Sent: 2016–04–25 11:07:00
From: dogdaygod@hmamail.com
To: besa@sigaint.org
Subject: Login failing

When I try to login now it is telling me no record found. Is your upgrade complete?

Sent: 2016–04–25 11:10:00
From: dogdaygod@hmamail.com
To: besa@sigaint.org
Subject: Account Status

Now it let me in, but my wallet is blank and my order it
blank

Sent: 2016–04–25 19:49:00
From: besa@sigaint.org
To: dogdaygod@hmamail.com
Subject: Re: Account Status

Hello,

We are still restoring from the backup; how many
bitcoins did you had? this will help us link your wallet to
your account

Your bitcoins are in your wallet and will show back up
on your balance

Let me know

Sent: 2016–04–25 20:39:00
From: dogdaygod@hmamail.com
To: besa@sigaint.org
Subject: Re: Re: Account Status

29.9 something. Do you need the exact amount or will that
get you close enough?

Sent: 2016–04–25 20:40:00
From: dogdaygod@hmamail.com
To: besa@sigaint.org
Subject: Re: Re: Account Status

Will I need to place the order again, or will that get linked up as well?

Sent: 2016–04–26 01:30:00
From: besa@sigaint.org
To: dogdaygod@hmamail.com
Subject: Re: Re: Re: Account Status

We found your wallet and imported it back into your account.

You should be able to view your balance now. Please let me know

Sent: 2016–04–26 01:30:00
From: besa@sigaint.org
To: dogdaygod@hmamail.com
Subject: Re: Re: Re: Account Status

Hello,

Yes, you will need to place the order again, it won't be restored from backup

Sent: 2016–04–27 03:28:00
From: dogdaygod@hmamail.com
To: besa@sigaint.org
Subject: Re: Re: Re: Re: Account Status

My Wallet was restored, but now it is gone again. The target is supposed to be alone tomorrow and the next day and I still do not have confirmation from you that someone is working on it.

Sent: 2016–04–27 14:03:00
From: besa@sigaint.org
To: dogdaygod@hmamail.com
Subject: Re: Re: Re: Re: Re: Account Status

I will check this and have it fixed.

Yes, I can confirm someone is working on it, hopefully tomorrow will be done

Sent: 2016–04–27 20:47:00
From: dogdaygod@hmamail.com
To: besa@sigaint.org
Subject: Re: Re: Re: Re: Re: Re: Account Status

OK, it looks like nothing was done on it today, if it is not done tomorrow (Thursday) then I want some evidence either picture or description that proves that they made an effort and that they have been tracking her. I am not convinced that anyone is actively working on the order.

Sent: 2016–04–27 21:54:00
From: dogdaygod@hmamail.com
To: besa@sigaint.org
Subject: Re: Re: Re: Re: Re: Re: Account Status

Got an update on her schedule tomorrow. She has class at Carver Lake Vet Center from 9:30–11:30 and should be home around noon, and has another class at 1:30, so best time would be to wait for her at home around noon, otherwise after the 1:30 class.

Sent: 2016–04–28 16:00:00
From: besa@sigaint.org
To: dogdaygod@hmamail.com
Subject: Re: Re: Re: Re: Re: Re: Re: Account Status

Hello,

I have restored your wallet, it dissapeared because an older copy of the database was restored and have interfered with wallets.

Please let me know if you see it

Regarding the job, we need to assign an well trained team to do it, they will do it with no delay

Sent: 2016–04–28 16:46:00
From: dogdaygod@hmamail.com
To: besa@sigaint.org
Subject: Re: Re: Re: Re: Re: Re: Re: Re: Account Status

When do you expect to have that team assigned. I was under the impression that a team was assigned. Also, you claim to have 24x7 support, but when I feed you information about her schedule and then I do not hear back from you for a day, then there is not enough time to get this information to the team to make use of it. I can get you guys good intel, but it needs to be able to be communicated quickly to be useful.

Sent: 2016–04–28 16:49:00
From: dogdaygod@hmamail.com
To: besa@sigaint.org
Subject: Re: Re: Re: Re: Re: Re: Re: Re: Account Status

Yes, I do see my wallet again.

Sent: 2016–04–28 16:54:00
From: besa@sigaint.org
To: dogdaygod@hmamail.com
Subject: Re: Re: Re: Re: Re: Re: Re: Re: Account Status

Hello,
    We reply times per day, we offer 24/7 support; the problem was that the existing team canceled the job, they won't do it.

We have to assign a well trained team. I am comunicating with several very skilled teams, they will travel to that location from a different state and do it; I will see which one accepts the job

Let me know

Sent: 2016–04–28 16:54:00
From: dogdaygod@hmamail.com
To: besa@sigaint.org
Subject: Re: Re: Re: Re: Re: Re: Re: Re: Account Status

Also to be clear, the schedule below is for today, it was sent last night. So It is noon here in about 5 minutes. So I doubt anyone could get there in time to be there before her afternoon class, but it should be relatively easy for someone to get there in 2 hours when her class is finished and do it right after that. This is a great deal for someone, no cameras, dead end street in the country, I do not see any way that there would be a witness, so it should be a clean get away, and a great payday for someone.

Sent: 2016–04–28 17:08:00
From: besa@sigaint.org
To: dogdaygod@hmamail.com
Subject: Re: Re: Re: Re: Re: Re: Re: Re: Re: Account Status

I spoke with a very experienced team that is well trained, they are one hour drive away of the location, but they ask for 40 BTC to do the job. :(

I tried to convince them that you will send extra money after the job is done, and that I trust you, but they have been done several hits and customers never send anything extra after the job is done.

I do not know what to say. If you can get some money from somewhere, I can assign this team, but I am afraid there is not enouch time to do it today.

If you can't get more money, is not a problem, I will find a different team that can do this

---

Sent: 2016–04–28 18:18:00
From: dogdaygod@hmamail.com
To: besa@sigaint.org
Subject: Re: Re: Re: Re: Re: Re: Re: Re: Re: Re: Account Status

Let's find a different team

Sent: 2016–04–28 19:12:00
From: dogdaygod@hmamail.com
To: besa@sigaint.org
Subject: Re: Re: Re: Re: Re: Re: Re: Re: Re: Re: Account Status

Call them one more time, because they could still make it today if they hurry. Tell them this. If I am telling the truth then they will end up 5BTC ahead of where they wanted to be, if I am a lying bitch then they will end up 10 BTC from where they wanted, but they will still be up 30BTC which is

better than 0 if you go with another team, and this will probably be one of the easiest 30BTC they can make. See if they
will do it with that reasoning. If not, then i guess we go with
another team.

Sent: 2016–04–30 01:49:00
From: dogdaygod@hmamail.com
To: besa@sigaint.org
Subject: Team

I assume the previous team declined. Have you found
someone new?

Sent: 2016–04–30 16:36:00
From: besa@sigaint.org
To: dogdaygod@hmamail.com
Subject: Re: Team

No, we din't found anyone new; most of our basic gang
members are not doing hits in the next weeks, and our
skilled hitman don't take the job unless they see at least 5
more btc on it

Sent: 2016–05–03 23:28:00
From: besa@sigaint.org
To: dogdaygod@hmamail.com
Subject: Re: Team

Hi,

Nothing new yet from the team; please let me know, we have three options

1. We can wait for the curent team to give status 2. We can assign a great team with experts that have military training; they become free two days ago from their past assigments in Europe; and they returned to USA, if you can add 8 bitcoin to your account 3. We can provide a refund

Either way is ok; I just give update

Sent: 2016–05–04 01:06:00
From: dogdaygod@hmamail.com
To: besa@sigaint.org
Subject: Re: Re: Team

I do not have the extra bit coins right now, so we can wait. It sounds like the husband is taking a trip with their child next week, and she will be alone 12th-17th. If someone freed up by then, then it would make it easy.

Sent: 2016–05–05 20:33:00
From: besa@sigaint.org
To: dogdaygod@hmamail.com
Subject: Re: Re: Re: Team

Hello,

Ok.

Let me know

Sent: 2016–05–07 02:32:00
From: dogdaygod@hmamail.com
To: besa@sigaint.org
Subject: Re: Re: Re: Re: Team

Yes, I was able to confirm that the husband is leaving out Thursday morning (12th), and will not be home until Tuesday evening (17th). This would be a great time, if you can find someone by then.

Sent: 2016–05–11 00:10:00
From: besa@sigaint.org
To: dogdaygod@hmamail.com
Subject: Re: Re: Re: Re: Re: Team

Hi,

Ok, this sounds like a great time and I have forwarded the info to the assigned hitman

He will do it as there should be a great oportunity

Sent: 2016–05–11 01:15:00
From: dogdaygod@hmamail.com
To: besa@sigaint.org
Subject: evidence

If it is not done by Sunday, then I would like some evidence (either description or photo) that shows that he has been tracking her and preparing.

Sent: 2016–05–11 17:03:00
From: besa@sigaint.org
To: dogdaygod@hmamail.com
Subject: Re: evidence

Hi, Ok, I forwarded them that request let me know

Sent: 2016–05–15 02:40:00
From: dogdaygod@hmamail.com
To: besa@sigaint.org
Subject: Half way through

We are half way through our current window, and I have not heard anything yet. If we miss this window, then I think it will be a while until we have another good window like this. I hope we do not miss out on her being alone for 5 full days and cannot make something happen.

Sent: 2016–05–17 02:54:00
From: dogdaygod@hmamail.com
To: besa@sigaint.org
Subject: Running short on time

It does not look like anything has happened yet, and I still have no evidence that she is even being tracked. I sounds like he will be out of town now until Thursday, but then this window will close AGAIN. Is your team going to fail again?

Sent: 2016–05–17 11:58:00
From: dogdaygod@hmamail.com
To: besa@sigaint.org
Subject: **Running short on time**

Please remind him that she is the primary target, and the house is secondary. At this point, if he does not think he can get the house, then have him focus on her. She is alone for the next couple days. Home would likely be the easiest place, but if somewhere else works better then do it when she is traveling somewhere.

Sent: 2016–05–17 21:25:00
From: dogdaygod@hmamail.com
To: besa@sigaint.org
Subject: **7x24 support**

You said that you have 7x24 support, but it looks like you have not read or responded to my messages and there is one in there from 2 days ago.

Sent: 2016–05–18 06:57:00
From: dogdaygod@hmamail.com
To: besa@sigaint.org

Subject: Refund

Just requested a refund. You guys have not been able to get this done. Which is sad. I expected more from you and the people that you contract with. I am not impressed with your organizations ability to hire quality individuals to do an easy task. I may reach out to you again if I have the additional funds for your high quality people, but until then I need the money back to keep what is left of my business running. I hope you guys have not screwed my business by letting this bitch live.

Sent: 2016–05–18 22:59:00
From: besa@sigaint.org
To: dogdaygod@hmamail.com
Subject: Re: Refund

Hello,
    we had some hard DDOS attacks to our website recently, that might have come from law enforcement organizations; we have been very bussy mitigation and resisting that; we worked to divert traffic that was from the ddos attack to other servers.
    now the attack is over and we are back on track
    the assigned hitman is on position and waiting for a better oportunity to do the hit
    let me know if you are sure you want to cancel, and we can send you a full refund, or if you want to continue and do this
    let me know

Sent: 2016–05–19 12:44:00
From: dogdaygod@hmamail.com
To: besa@sigaint.org
Subject: Re: Re: Refund

If he can do it, then do it.

Sent: 2016–05–19 14:34:00
From: dogdaygod@hmamail.com
To: besa@sigaint.org
Subject: Job

He had a full week to do this job. It is awful that he waits until the last day. If he can do it today, then he can do it otherwise we will need to cancel. I did get a call from the target and it sounds like she will still be alone today until about 4PM Central time, so it would have to be done by then. So tell him it is 29BTC or 0, and he has about 6 hours to get it done.

Sent: 2016–05–19 17:51:00
From: dogdaygod@hmamail.com
To: besa@sigaint.org
Subject: 3 hours left

Based on my info, He only has 3 hours left and it does not look like you are reading these and forwarding on the information. He needs to hurry or he will get NOTHING.

Sent: 2016–05–19 19:02:00
From: dogdaygod@hmamail.com
To: besa@sigaint.org
Subject: 2 Hours left

It still does not look like you are reading these and communicating with him.

Sent: 2016–05–19 19:54:00
From: besa@sigaint.org
To: dogdaygod@hmamail.com
Subject: Re: 2 Hours left

Hello,
    I read the comunication and forwarded it to him.
    He saith he will do it.
    Let me know

Sent: 2016–05–19 20:02:00
From: dogdaygod@hmamail.com
To: besa@sigaint.org
Subject: Re: Re: 2 Hours left

Excellent. If this finally works I will owe you one.

Sent: 2016–05–19 21:37:00
From: dogdaygod@hmamail.com
To: besa@sigaint.org
Subject: **A little more time**

I just talked with her, which means it is not done yet. NOT GOOD, but it looks like the husband was slowed down and will not be in until about midnight, so it looks like there is a little more time, but not much.

Sent: 2016–05–20 17:17:00
From: dogdaygod@hmamail.com
To: besa@sigaint.org
Subject: **Cancel and Refund**

That's it, your local guys suck. They cannot do simple things even when given plenty of time. I will try again later with one of your pros, but I will need to save up for that. Can you give me a quote of what I would need to work with a pro and then I will try to get a new order worked up in a couple months. Until then please refund my money. I put the request into the wallet. Let me know if you need anything else.

Sent: 2016–05–20 19:45:00
From: besa@sigaint.org
To: dogdaygod@hmamail.com

Subject: Re: Cancel and Refund

Hi,

I am sorry to dissapoint you.

Unfortunattely, this site has been hacked. We got all customer and target information and we will send it to to law enforcement unless you send 10 bitcoin to this address 1H1pNNP6dqWuk9H3EKfGjFTc7grasd9D2X

We injected mallware and javascript into the site and are able to dox the customers (find out who they are) by expert IP and proxy analisis and this hacked site uses javascript to extract personal information from the user computer.

if you want to avoid us give your info and target info to law enforcement, please send us 10 Bitcoin to the address above

Once we receive the additional money, we will delete your account, all messages, and all information about you and the target.

If you don't send the additonal money, we will send all information to law enforcement and you might be arrested, ordering murder and paying for murder can get you in jail for a long time

you have one week to send the money to the above address, or you go to jail, we have extracted everything from your computer and have complex info on you along with all proofs that you ordered the hit, purchased bitcoin, sent bitcoins to the address of besa mafia, and provided target details, this should get you in jail if you don't pay up

if you say you don't have the money, please borrow it, if you can't borrow it then you go jail please do not post anything about us blackmailing you anywhere, if you do, we will immediately send your information to law enforcement

let me know

BLACK DEATH GROUP WEBSITE

Transcription of selected pages of the Black Death Group website

Homepage

We are Black Death, an organized crime group based in Eastern Europe. We specialize in all highly profitable services that are of our interest and capabilities. Content you will find here will be highly disturbing for a majority of our

society, we deal with those who don't give a shit.

Services we provide include:

- **Mercenary** (service with low availability)
- **Assassins** (service with moderate availability)
- **Image Destruction** (service with high availability)
- **Bombing** (service)
- **New Identity** (service)
- **Drugs dealing** (sales)
- **Arms and explosives dealing** (sales)
- **Heavy arms dealing** (sales and auctions)
- **Trafficking** (auctions)

Payment and terms can be found here.

Recruitment if you wish to work for us. We expect the best, but we also give the best.

Contact us to discuss any other needs, please note that some of the services above may take some time, always make sure to check appropriate calendar for either Mercenary or Assassination service.

TRAFFICKING

All our girls are set for auctions only and are being held in Europe. If you wish, we can ladnap a specific target for your needs. That service will be rather expensive, especially for targets outside Europe.

-All the details, including age, name, nationality, and measurements are in the girl's profile.

- We have a doctor contractor who tests girls for the sexually transmitted diseases, and whether they are pure

- Girl is only pure if the profile says so.

- Girls can be transported globally. We have contractors for that for a price.

- EU delivery is free of charge.

In order to take part in an auction, you need to contact us and indicate which girl, or girls, you are interested in. You will then be provided with the link to the auction. You know the drill. And should this be your first auction, you will have to be able to prove you know someone who previously dealt with us. You will then be briefed about the process.

This service is strictly only for the recommended people. We do not sell girls to anyone who is not aware of the rules, new people only come look asked too many questions and are generally time wasters

Upcoming auctions

[NAME REDACTED]
   Caucasian
   born in UK
   17, years old.
   34-24-34
   brunette,
   asking price $120,000
   auction takes place, 22.05.2016

[NAME REDACTED]
   Caucasian
   Born in UK
   15 years old.
   34-24-32
   brunette
   PURE!
   Asking price $750,000
   Auction takes place. 29.05.2016
   <u>AUCTION FOR [*] IS FULLY BOOKED</u>

[NAME REDACTED]
   Caucasian - tanned
   born in Spain,
   19, years old.
   38-24-32

Brunette,
Fitness, implants,
asking price $250,000
Auction takes place, 05.06.2016.

Source: Europol

ALSO BY EILEEN ORMSBY

Psycho.com (Dark Webs Book 1)

Murder on the Dark Web (Dark Webs Book 2)

Stalkers (Dark Webs Book 3)

Little Girls Lost (Dark Webs Book 4)

The Darkest Web

Silk Road

Keep going for sneak peeks of these books

PLEA FROM THE AUTHOR

Thank you for choosing to read my books. It means everything that you have given me your valuable time to share these stories with you.

I am truly blessed to have such a fulfilling job, but I only have that job because of people like you; people kind enough to give my books a chance and spend their hard earned money buying them. For that I am eternally grateful.

If you would like to find out more about my other books then please visit my website for full details.

You can find it at: www.EileenOrmsby.com

Also feel free to contact me on Twitter, Facebook or via email (all details on the website) as I would love to hear from you.

If you enjoyed this book and would like to help, then you could think about leaving a review on Amazon, Goodreads, or anywhere else that readers visit.

The most important part of how well a book sells is how many positive reviews it has, so if you leave me one then you are directly helping me to continue on this journey as a full-time writer.

Thank you in advance to anyone who does.

PSYCHO.COM
DARK WEBS BOOK 1

A pair of teens go on a murderous rampage and their exploits are immortalised in the most shocking video ever to circulate the internet, "3 Guys, 1 Hammer"

A serial killer with over 100 kills to his name walks free and becomes a Youtube sensation

A psychopath lures victims through online dating to use as "research" for his twisted film project

Serial killers have been with us for decades.

The internet has put them in our pockets.

Psycho.com is a chilling look at what happens when murderous minds meet modern technology.

Available from all major retailers

STALKERS
DARK WEBS BOOK 3

A bookworm teenager is brutally attacked by a vengeful author after she gives him a scathing review. She could never have known that his book was a fictionalised confession of years of pathological stalking of a young woman whose mistake was to smile at him.

A young Hollywood starlet enjoys rising fame on a smash-hit sitcom, unaware that her greatest fan is an unhinged teenager hell-bent on meeting his crush... until she films a love scene and his adoration turns into a quest to see her punished.

A 15-year-old boy is surprised when MI6 approaches him online with a direct order from the Queen to work as a spy. His exciting new life takes a deadly turn when his girlfriend is kidnapped and he is ordered to kill his best friend

Dark Webs Book 3 takes you into the twisted world of stalkers and the devastating impact their obsessions can have on their victims

Available from all major retailers

LITTLE GIRLS LOST
DARK WEBS BOOK 4

A 12-year-old girl never makes it home from a Halloween party. When the people of the town discover what was done to her, they cancel Halloween until the real monsters who roam their streets can be caught.

A 14-year-old girl is excited to attend her first evening party with local teens. What happens there is every parent's nightmare, but it is made infinitely worse when the residents of the town close ranks around the perpetrators.

A schoolgirl comes to the aid of a middle-aged woman who has lost her puppy and becomes the victim of the most hated couple in Australian history.

Police tell gang members a 16-year-old girl has agreed to testify against them, with predictable results. When they make an arrest for her murder, a Hollywood sitcom plays a surprising role in the outcome

Available from all major retailers

Eileen Ormsby has spent the past five years exploring every corner of the Dark Web. She has shopped on darknet markets, contributed to forums, waited in red rooms and been threatened by hitmen on murder-for-hire sites. On occasions, her dark web activities have poured out into the real world and she has attended trials, met with criminals and the law enforcement who tracked them down, interviewed dark web identities and visited them in prison.

This book will take you into the murkiest depths of the web's dark underbelly: a place of hitmen for hire, red rooms, hurtcore sites and markets that will sell anything a person is willing to pay for - including another person. The Darkest Web.

Available from all major retailers

Silk Road

It was the 'eBay of drugs', a billion dollar empire. Behind it was the FBI's Most Wanted Man, a mysterious crime czar dubbed 'Dread Pirate Roberts'. SILK ROAD lay at the heart of the 'Dark Web' - a parallel internet of porn, guns, assassins and drugs. Lots of drugs. With the click of a button LSD, heroin, meth, coke, any illegal drug imaginable, would wing its way by regular post from any dealer to any user in the world. How was this online drug cartel even possible? And who was the mastermind all its low roads led to? This is the incredible true story of Silk Road's rise and fall, told with unparalleled insight into the main players - including alleged founder and kingpin Dread Pirate Roberts himself - by lawyer and investigative journalist Eileen Ormsby. A stunning crime story with a truth that explodes off the page.

Available from all major retailers

REFERENCES AND ACKNOWLEDGEMENTS

The Amy Allwine story was all original research, with my personal attendance at the trial of Stephen Allwine and full access to all police and court documents. I also personally interviewed police, prosecutors, hackers, the owner of Besa Mafia, and friends of Amy. I owe special thanks to the people of Cottage Grove, in particular the friends of Amy and the Cottage Grove police department, with a special shoutout to Randy McAlister and Jared Landkamer for their time and insights.

Thanks to Lorna Hendry for the stellar editing job on this book

Chris Monteiro has covered Besa Mafia extensively on his website at Pirate.London

Chloe Ayling's story was covered by multiple news outlets and I referred to more articles and interviews than I could ever possibly reference. Special mention should be made to:

Ayling, Chloe *Kidnapped - The Untold Story of My Abduction*, Kings Road Publishing, 2018

Chloe Ayling's statement to Italian police (reprinted in full in *The Sun* https://www.thesun.co.uk/news/4207316/chloe-ayling-model-kidnap-italy-black-death-dark-web/)

Green, Phil *Confessions of a model agent*, self-published 2018

Made in United States
Orlando, FL
01 September 2023

36620419R00169